American Political Cartoons

The Evolution of a National Identity, 1754-2010

Jeff Danziger, *Christian Science Monitor*, circa 1990.

American Political Cartoons

The Evolution of a National Identity, 1754-2010

Stephen Hess and Sandy Northrop

With a new chapter by the authors

Routledge
Taylor & Francis Group
LONDON AND NEW YORK

Originally published in 1996 by Elliot & Clark Publishing

Published 2011 by Transaction Publishers

Published 2017 by Routledge
2 Park Square, Milton Park, Abingdon, Oxon OX14 4RN
711 Third Avenue, New York, NY 10017, USA

Routledge is an imprint of the Taylor & Francis Group, an informa business

Library of Congress Catalog Number: 2010025038

Library of Congress Cataloging-in-Publication Data

Hess, Stephen.
American political cartoons : from 1754-2010 / Stephen Hess and Sandy Northrop.
p. cm.
Originally published: Montgomery, Ala. : Elliott & Clark Pub., 1996.
Includes bibliographical references and index.
ISBN 978-1-4128-1119-4 (alk. paper)
1. Political cartoons--United States--History--19th century. 2. Political cartoons--United States--History--20th century. 3. United States--Politics and government--Caricatures and cartoons. 4. American wit and humor, Pictorial. I. Northrop, Sandy, 1947- II. Hess, Stephen. Drawn & quartered. III. Title.

NC1425.H47 2010
320.97302'07--dc22

2010025038

ISBN 13: 978-1-4128-1119-4 (pbk)

For Dave and Beth

for their abiding love and support

William Walker (1871–1938), *Life*, February 21, 1907.

CONTENTS

INTRODUCTION

"STOP THEM DAMN PICTURES," demanded William M. Tweed of his cohorts. "I don't care so much what the papers write about me. My constituents can't read. But, damn it, they can see pictures."

"Boss" Tweed was head of Tammany Hall, the political machine that had run the city of New York since 1789. His outburst was inspired by a cartoon in the August 19, 1871, issue of *Harper's Weekly*, in which he and his three chief cronies—Peter B. "Brains" Sweeny, Richard B. "Slippery Dick" Connolly, and New York Mayor A. Oakey "O.K." Hall—are shown pointing to one another in response to the question "Who stole the people's money?" Their theft from the city's treasury was estimated at $200 million.

Thomas Nast (1840-1902), *Harper's Weekly*, August 19, 1871.

Tweed wanted to stop the cartoons of Thomas Nast, who for four months had been drawing a scathing series attacking him. A Tammany henchman was sent to Nast's home with an offer of $100,000 to "study art" in Europe.

"Do you think I could get two hundred thousand?" asked the $5,000-a-year artist.

"Well, possibly.... You have a great talent."

Curious to see how high a price his talent could command, Nast told biographer Albert Bigelow Paine he bid up Tweed's emissary to a half-million dollars. Then, he cut off the negotiations. "I don't think I'll go to Europe," he said. Nast's subsequent campaign against the Tweed Ring, the most incisive in the history of American political cartooning, receives greater attention later in our story. But the result sets the stage for a look at the political cartoon's role in the American democratic dialogue.

On July 1, 1876, after five years of Nast's cartoons had brought Tammany Hall corruption to the attention of the city, he pictured Tweed in a prison-stripe suit holding two street urchins by their collars. The cartoon suggested that Tammany Hall's attempt to reform its scandal-riddled administration had consisted of nothing more than arresting the most humble culprits, while the major criminals remained at large. It contained the familiar likeness of Tweed, who had escaped from jail and fled to Spain.

Soon after, a cable from Vigo, Spain, stated that "Twid" had been apprehended for kidnapping two American children. A Spanish official who did not read English had spotted

HARPER'S WEEKLY. A JOURNAL OF CIVILIZATION.

Vol. XX.—No. 1018.] NEW YORK, SATURDAY, JULY 1, 1876. [WITH A SUPPLEMENT. PRICE TEN CENTS.

POLITICAL "CAPITAL."

The "people are in a very puzzled and despondent state of mind about the political situation, and have got beyond the point at which they look for the appearance of the ideal statesman uniting the purest motives with the highest ability. They can get the pure motives, and they can get the high ability; but somehow, owing to no matter what circumstances, to get a man who unites both into a leading place in the government is a work of such difficulty that most people have given it up as (for the present at least) a bad job, and are willing to content themselves with any man who, for whatever motive, will do good work. It so happens, too, that the work to be done at this moment is not work which calls either for the highest order of genius or the highest aspirations. A man may do it very well without being a Moses or a Washington—without, in short, being either a prophet or a hero. He has neither to lead a race out of captivity nor call a nation into existence. The task before the American politician of to-day is the simple and somewhat homely one of preventing public officers from stealing and dividing the public money, and of preventing the government from cheating its creditors; and when a man offers himself for this work, there is no general disposition to ask whether he is a statesman of the first rank, or whether his political judgment has always been sure or his voice been always heard on the right side. In fact, they go so far as to say that to make capital in this way is a good thing to do, and they wish all politicians to engage in it. They are ready to forbear all curious inquiries into the motives or antecedents of men who will undertake to put an end to cheating and stealing. In fact, the voters of the country are sticking notices up offering the highest offices in their gift, and "no questions asked," to any body who will bring in a few plunderers of the state. Mr. Tilden has achieved his present success simply owing to his having, before any body else of his class, understood the exact nature of the situation. He perceived sooner than his competitors that the time had come to stop preaching, and to begin making arrests and drawing up indictments. He now finds, and his competitors find, that his acuteness has rendered him the highest service, and his enemies actually play into his hands."—*The Nation*, October 7, 1875.

TWEED-LE-DEE AND TILDEN-DUM.

Reform Tweed. "If all the people want is to have somebody arrested, I'll have you plunderers convicted. You will be allowed to escape; nobody will be hurt; and then Tilden will go to the White House, and I to Albany as Governor."

Thomas Nast,
***Harper's Weekly*,**
July 1, 1876.

Tweed from the *Harper's Weekly* cartoon, and, while he assumed the wrong crime, his identification was flawless. Legend has it that Tweed's baggage contained a complete set of the Nast cartoons. Boss Tweed was returned to New York City's Ludlow Street Jail, where he occupied the warden's parlor at $75 a week. He died there on April 12, 1878.

Nast's crusade against the Tweed Ring remains the tale most often told to reinforce the power of the cartoon. But like many legends, the story is largely apocryphal. Despite the cartoon series' enormous popularity—*Harper's Weekly* circulation tripled in 1871—it did not bring down New York's Democratic Party machine. Tweed actually won reelection and before long Tammany Hall was back doing business as usual. Boss Tweed was no more responsible for the pillage of city funds than his cohorts, but Thomas Nast singled him out because of his physical attributes, stretching Tweed's nose and inflating his belly until the politician took on sinister proportions and thus became a living symbol of corruption.

The mythic power of cartoons has continued to grow since Thomas Nast took on William Tweed, placing the cartoonists' role in an exalted position as a standard-bearer for integrity and truth in journalism, as the voice of common sense—the boy revealing that the emperor has no clothes. The cartoonists' influence may be illusory but their popularity is not. The way in which they are able to reduce a complex issue to a simple cartoon presented in a tiny box—often no bigger than three by five inches—has delighted and mystified American readers for nearly two centuries. It has also involved them, if only vicariously, in the political process. Although today's cartoons take many different stylistic forms, they stand out amidst the information glut in newspapers, magazines, television, silently but humorously commanding us to peruse their point of view. "Good cartoons are like visual rock and roll," wrote *Newsday* cartoonist Doug Marlette. "They hit you primitively and emotionally. There is something wild and untamed about the best of them, raw and vaguely threatening like Little Richard or Jerry Lee Lewis...A cartoon cannot say, 'On the other hand,' and it cannot defend itself. It is a frontal assault, a slam dunk, a cluster bomb."

Put today's cartoonists together in a room and you will find a sea of 200 casually clad white males, their ranks interrupted with only an occasional flash of skirt or alternate skin tone. Most cheerfully admit to being social misfits in their early days: a stutterer, nerd, or general adolescent ne'er-do-well who used his or her quick-draw humor to win friends and gain notoriety. "As a child," recalls cartoonist Jules Feiffer, "the only thing I wanted to be was grown up. Because I was a terrible flop as a child. You cannot be a successful boy in America if you cannot throw or catch a ball." Many never grew up. Mike Peters of the *Dayton Daily News* once jumped through a window into an editorial meeting dressed in the Superman costume his wife had made him. "Sorry I'm late," he announced. "The weather was lousy over Cleveland."

Most cartoonists today studied art and apprenticed on college newspapers, unlike their predecessors who had little formal art training and were largely self-taught. *The Masses'* Robert Minor worked for the railroads laying track before discovering he could make a living cartooning; Herbert Johnson, cartoonist for the *Saturday Evening Post,* worked initially as a clerk, a stenographer, and a bookkeeper. All cartoonists love their profession. Most are workaholics; some are double dippers who produce both a daily editorial cartoon and a daily cartoon strip.

Cartoonists come from divergent beliefs and backgrounds, and their politics sweep the spectrum. Although most cartoonists today are liberal and align themselves with the Democratic Party, in the nineteenth century the Republican and conservative perspectives were more likely to be represented in political cartoons. Whatever their political ideology, these satirists all have had a point of view, and they are bound together by a driving need to put their own spin on the world around them. And this is what makes a good cartoon.

"JUST GIMME A COUPLA ASPIRIN, I ALREADY GOT A PURPLE HEART."

Bill Mauldin (1921-2003),
***Stars and Stripes*, December 1943.**

A good cartoon is unabashedly subjective. It represents an opinion. "I've always operated off of my peculiar sort of moral base, and I set everything that happens in the world against my own standards of what I think is right and wrong," said Bill Mauldin. When, as a young cartoonist and soldier on the World War II battlefront, Mauldin depicted the less-than-heroic life of Willie and Joe, two battle-weary soldiers, he flew in the face of convention. War had generally been portrayed as heroic; battles were fought and depicted as great moral crusades. Mauldin's tired soldiers conveyed a more realistic image.

"I HAVE HERE IN MY HAND—"

Herbert Block (1909-2001),
***Washington Post*, May 7, 1954.**

The cartoons of Herbert Block, a.k.a. Herblock, also reflected their creator's insistent search for the essence of a situation over a career spanning sixty years. In the early 1950s he attacked Senator Joseph McCarthy, who had embarked on a hunt for domestic Communists, claiming they had infiltrated every level of government. Over a four-year period, Block's cartoons helped peel away the politician's fabrications and expose the hypocrisy, challenging readers to question McCarthy's motives and reexamine their own Cold War fears. The most important part of every cartoon is the idea that drives it. Rollin Kirby, one of the finest American newspaper cartoonists of the twentieth century, said that a good cartoon consists of 75 percent idea and 25 percent drawing. "A good idea has carried many an indifferent drawing to glory," commented Kirby in 1918, "but never has a good drawing rescued a bad idea from oblivion." David

David Levine (1926-2009), *The New York Review of Books*, May 12, 1966.

Levine's caricature of Lyndon Johnson at the time when the Vietnam War threatened to overwhelm his presidency used simple juxtaposition to create a searing portrait. At a press briefing, Johnson had pulled up his shirt to show reporters his scar from a recent gallbladder operation. Levine changed just a single detail of the actual event: he drew the scar in the shape of Vietnam.

The great cartoonists have achieved lasting recognition because they have a political or social point of view and have kept that perspective continually before the audience, constantly inventing new ways to present the same message. Would Thomas Nast have been successful in exposing Tammany Hall's corruption if he had just drawn one cartoon? Daniel Fitzpatrick, one of the masters in the use of symbolism, transformed Nazi Germany's swastika into a horrific death machine. As Adolf Hitler's armies marched across Europe in the 1930s, Fitzpatrick used his symbol repeatedly to challenge Americans to rethink their isolationist stand and enter World War II.

Symbols are only one of the weapons in a cartoonist's highly manipulative language, a visual language that is as sophisticated as any word-driven vehicle. "Although political cartoons usually achieve greatness in their simplicity in theme and graphics, it is not a simple medium," remarked historian Roger Fischer. "In less than ten seconds, the skilled cartoonist must establish audience recognition of his or her visual symbol, make a political statement, and sell newspapers or magazines." Although the style of cartoons has changed from the ballooned, multipeopled woodcuts and engravings of the nineteenth century to the simple pen-and-ink sketches we call cartoons today, the use of juxtaposition of pictures and words, caricatures and symbols, remains largely unchanged.

"NEXT!"

Daniel Fitzpatrick (1891-1939), *St. Louis Post-Dispatch*, August 24, 1939.

DOWN TO BOTTOMLESS PERDITION

Daniel Fitzpatrick, *St. Louis Post-Dispatch*, May 7, 1945.

The imagery in cartoons changes to fit the times, often using allusions to literary works. In the nineteenth century, American high and lowbrows shared the same classics that included the Scriptures, the epics of Homer, the fables of Aesop, the plays of Shakespeare, *Don Quixote*, and *Oliver Twist*, and cartoonists drew upon the familiar characters they offered. Any random sampling of that century's cartoons is sure to turn up Lincoln as Othello or Tweed as Falstaff. Paul Conrad is one of the few American cartoonists to successfully employ Shakespearean analogy in contemporary cartooning. In a series done during the last days of the Nixon administration, Conrad portrayed the troubled president as both Hamlet and Richard II. Today's cartoonists more often rely on television, movie, and advertising imagery for their symbols, which have a shorter shelf life. Mickey Mouse and Superman will undoubtedly be icons for

Homer Davenport (1867-1912),
***New York Journal*, July 6, 1899.**

the next generation, but what of the Duracell Rabbit (who "keeps on going and going") or Forrest Gump's box of chocolates?

The situations in which cartoons take place change, too. P. T. Barnum's museum in New York City was a popular attraction in the mid-1800s, and cartoonists used its distinctive surroundings to depict politicians as members of Barnum's freak show. Today, a cartoon's setting is much simpler and certainly less sensational. Many cartoons take place around the family television set where most Americans get their news.

Cartoonists are the first to admit that they can't compete with television's or photography's ability to impart information. A cartoonist's job is not to present the news but to interpret it. As *Chicago Tribune* cartoonist Jeff MacNelly said, "A political cartoon is not like a truckload of tomatoes in 90 degree weather. It isn't something that has to be delivered the next day." Cartoons can visualize abstract ideas and complex emotions, something that neither photographs nor television can do. Scott Long, a cartoonist for the *Minneapolis Tribune,* once said, "The photographer deals with physical objects. Ask a photographer to take a picture of the Dollar Gap or the New Deal or the Great Leap Forward or the Separation of Church and State and he will be baffled." Cartoonists continually translate political abstractions into tangible visual representations.

Cartoons work best when they attack. With the rare exception of applauding a peace agreement or a singular individual act of valor, cartoonists are nobody's cheerleaders. Some cartoonists gauge their success by the hate mail they receive.

Put to work all the elements that shape a cartoon and you have a powerful tool: a good cartoon is so simple, so straightforward, it seems to speak an inherent truth. Bernard Reilly, formerly of the Library of Congress, notes that the public often perceives the cartoonist "as a candid observer of his society who, from a vantage point above the political fray, exposes

Mike Peters, *Dayton Daily News*, 1983.

Tony Auth, ***Philadelphia Inquirer*, September 21, 1976.**

THE NATIONAL DIME-MUSEUM

Bernard Gillam (1859-1896), *Puck*, April 15, 1884.

foibles of public figures and public life." It is a viewpoint Reilly does not agree with, however, for the cartoonist is human after all, and just as likely to be swayed by the same tendencies: a personal political agenda, an inflated sense of self-importance, a hypocritical point of view, or a desire to perpetuate the status quo.

"Cartoons claim to be peddling truth," writes political cartoon analyst Charles Press, "but what they are giving us are their assumptions of reality. The political cartoon has always been an aesthetic achievement only by accident. "Its purpose is propaganda, not art." The censors in France in 1835 feared the potential of the picture so much that when the September Censorship Decree was written, far greater restrictions were put on images than words. In the United States during World War I, a government agency was organized in Washington to mobilize the power of the cartoon, with the result that some cartoonists became little more than government propagandists.

Cartoons have been an ingredient in American politics since the 1828 presidential election when the fiery populist Andrew Jackson squared off in a rematch with President John Quincy Adams. The illustrated journals and daily newspapers of the nineteenth century were openly partisan, and the few cartoons that appeared were designed to convince voters that their candidates and their positions were the best.

Partisan publications are still with us. Although today's papers tend toward balanced reporting, it's generally no secret which party they support. Most cartoonists work for publications that have a viewpoint they agree with: Herbert Block was a Democrat and worked for a liberal newspaper, the *Washington Post,* Wayne

Stayskal is a Republican and makes the more conservative *Tampa Tribune* his base; Jules Feiffer's radical politics dovetailed with his employer of many years, the *Village Voice.* Both Don Wright of the *Palm Beach Post* and the *Philadelphia Inquirer's* Tony Auth take an active interest in their paper's stand on issues. Auth sits in on weekly editorial meetings; Wright often reads newspaper copy before it is set.

HUGGING A DELUSION

Laura Foster, *Life*, November 11, 1915.

Whether or not there is a marriage of political beliefs between cartoonist and editor, most cartoonists' work now appears as independent commentary in their newspapers. When Paul Conrad's cartoons were moved from the editorial page to the op-ed page of the *Los Angeles Times* during the Watergate investigation, Conrad and many other cartoonists opposed the repositioning, fearing that the new placement, if it became a trend, would diminish the status of their work. That sentiment has long since disappeared. "I think the move to op-ed was the best thing that ever happened, because now there's none of this nonsense about who speaks for the *Times,"* Conrad said. "We agreed ... that if a cartoon works, if it isn't libelous, and is in good taste, so be it. This is Ol' Con talking, not the *Times."*

In gaining autonomy cartoonists are—in theory—now free to comment on whatever they choose. But any cartoon-loving reader has to be wary of the restrictions a newspaper, which exists to make a profit, might impose on cartoons and cartoonists. Cartoons on local issues can hit a paper's economic base, and many publishers remain watchful for cartoons that could impede their potential revenue or annoy a local politician. Paul Szep remembers

George Fisher (1923-2003),
***Arkansas Gazette*, March 2, 1977.**

when, after a series of cartoons on Massachusetts Governor Edward King, the *Boston Globe* was sued for libel. Szep's editors stood behind him. "My goodness, a political cartoonist holding up a politician for ridicule...That's not libel, that's a job description," his editor said. The paper eventually won the legal battle, but a substantial amount of money was spent on Szep's defense. "They never told me to desist," he remembered, "but the next time a situation like that occurred, I had to ask my-self: do I want to put us through that again?"

National syndication plays a large role in the business of cartoons. Syndicates decide whose cartoons will be distributed nationally and, thereby, which cartoonists will become widely known. Today's audience knows Garry Trudeau's "*Doonesbury*" because it has been running for 40 years and is syndicated in more than 1,500 papers; but George Fisher, who worked for the *Arkansas Gazette,* never received national recognition because he focused on regional issues. Fisher's attack on the U.S. Army Corps of Engineers in Arkansas in the early 1970s helped halt needless plans for damming several of the state's rivers. There are countless other cartoonists who have influenced local issues over the years whose names are not household words.

Many issues have also gone unnoted, or were reported from only one point of view, because their spokespersons had no access to the mainstream press. As the question of women's suffrage gained strength in the late 1800s and early 1900s, the suffragettes and their cause found few journalists or cartoonists willing to take up their cause. Similarly, few cartoons were penned from the African American perspective. But a black press grew up in Northern cities after the Civil War that had its own cartoonists, many of whom drew powerful indictments of the discrimination and drama surrounding their daily lives. Only recently has the work of cartoonists such as Oliver Harrington, who started cartooning in Harlem in the 1930s and had a career lasting nearly sixty years, reached a broader audience.

The most negative impact cartoonists have had over the years is when they intentionally set out to demean various segments of American society. Caricature is built on distortion of recognizable traits, but many cartoonists in the nineteenth century built cruel stereotypes that had no factual basis. African Americans have suffered the greatest injustices from mis-

"HERE, BROTHER BOOTSIE, TAKE THIS EXTRA HAMMER I GOT HERE IN CASE THE GENTLEMENS OF THE LAW DECIDES THAT THIS DEMONSTRATION IS *TOO* PEACEFUL!"

Oliver Harrington (1911-95), circa 1960.

DARKTOWN ATHLETICS: A QUARTER MILE DASH

Thomas Worth (1859-1996), *Currier & Ives*, 1893.

DARKTOWN BOWLING: CLUB BOWLED OUT

Thomas Worth, *Currier & Ives*, 1888.

representation in cartoons. Thomas Worth's "Darktown" series for Currier & Ives is one telling example. "Americans probably regarded Worth's Darktown series as good-natured, comic entertainments," said historian John Appel. "From today's vantage point ... they are vicious, thoughtless lampoons of African Americans as clumsy fools and clowns, without common sense and the capacity to feel pain, hurt or embarrassment."

Yet every newly arrived immigrant group, particularly the Irish and the Jews, was greeted with hostile depictions in magazines, newspapers, and minstrel shows in the years following the Civil War, when racial stereotypes became staple ingredients of American culture. Thomas Nast drew cruel monkey-like caricatures of the Irish in the same pages of *Harper's Weekly* in which he had been knighted for waging battle with Tammany Hall. Nast and *Puck's* cartoonist Joseph Keppler, both immigrants and Catholics by birth, used malicious metaphors to undermine the growth of the Catholic Church in their adopted land. These views were supported by their readers: America's middle class.

For better or for worse, cartoonists capture the popular sentiment and culture of their times often more truthfully—certainly more colorfully—than a scholar's textbook. Historian Daniel Boorstin argued that too often history is written using only academic references and fails to take advantage of the popular periodicals of the day. He offers the *Davy Crockett Almanacs* as one example. Fifty of these cheap, throwaway paperbacks were

December 9, 1876

The Ignorant Vote—Honors Are Easy.

Thomas Nast, *Harper's Weekly*, December 9, 1876.

POPE LEO XIII.—A PHYSIOGNOMICAL STUDY.

Joseph Keppler (1838-94), *Puck*, April 24, 1878.

produced between 1836 and 1856. They told tales of Crockett's adventures and were read, carried in saddlebags, and traded around the campfires as America moved West. Few copies of the almanacs remain, and their importance in shaping America at that moment has gone unnoticed.

Political cartoons share a similar fate: once they were tacked on tavern walls; today they are hung on refrigerator doors, copied, e-mailed, and eventually forgotten. Yet these cartoons vibrantly reflect their moment in time: the costumes and conversations, the prejudices and fears. While a cartoon's popularity may prove ephemeral, cartoons will survive as clues to our society's interests, beliefs, and values—both positive and negative. For *Economist* cartoonist Kevin Kallaugher, political cartoons are like magnifying glasses: "A hundred years from now when historians look at our cartoons, they can say 'that was the dilemma facing the cartoonist that day.' Cartoons reflect something that no other historical artifact can reveal."

Grant Hamilton (1862-1926), *Judge*, July 9, 1898.

"IT SEEMS THERE WASN'T ANY DEPRESSION AT ALL"

Daniel Fitzpatrick, *St. Louis Post-Dispatch*, December 18, 1935.

"DON'T MIND ME—JUST GO RIGHT ON TALKING"

Herbert Block, *Washington Post*, January 1, 1949.

"OK, THEN!—BUT IF THIS RUNS JUST ONE SECOND INTO THE CLEVELAND-DALLAS GAME ..."

ABOVE: Pat Oliphant, *Denver Post* December 19, 1968.

RIGHT: Jeff Danzinger, *Christian Science Monitor*, 1990's.

These five cartoons document public sentiment concerning: the U.S. invasion of Cuba, 1896; the Great Depression, 1935;the proliferation of atomic weaponry, 1949; the NASA space program, 1968; and the rising cost of health care, circa 1990.

Today's cartoonists often abide by the unofficial rules of political correctness, a policy they publicly decry. But each era has produced its list of dos and don'ts, and the ebb and flow of what is or is not socially acceptable has produced laughable hypocrisies. British cartoonist David Low once said, "The limitation imposed by the necessity of conforming to the genteel code of taboos which institute the average man's 'good taste' are such that they cramp the style of any satirist worth his salt. Social polish, courtesy, and urbanity merely to soothe sensitive feelings are no part of the technique of true satire.... The caricaturist, be he right or wrong, must be individual or languish. Caricature must be a critic of the social system, not its servant." Pat Oliphant, one of the most outspoken cartoonists in articulating the need to use the cartoon for critical comment, agrees: "Our business is valuable enough to be looked upon as a leading vehicle for pointed and savage opinion and someone will always be offended."

Victims of cartoons often decry the images that lampoon them. Some have gone so far as to try to legislate what imagery a cartoonist can use. One politician who felt himself particularly discriminated against by

"It may well be doubted whether ever before in the history of American politics such an event (as my nomination) has occurred."—FROM JUDGE PENNYPACKER'S RECENT SPEECH AT THE ACADEMY OF MUSIC.

Charles Nolan (1859-1904), *Philadelphia North American*, October 19, 1902.

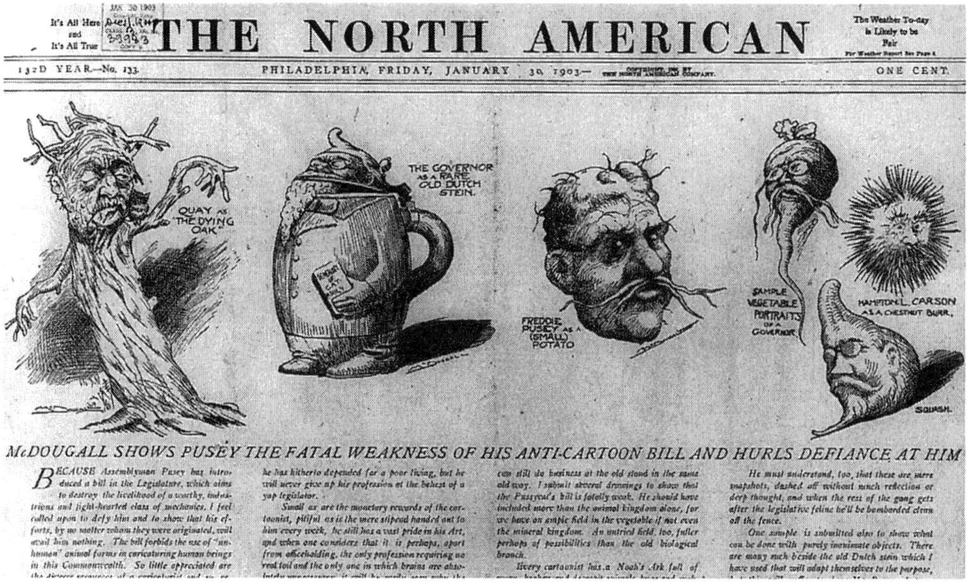

Walt McDougall (1858-1938), *Philadelphia North American*, January 30, 1903.

the cartoonists was Samuel Pennypacker of Pennsylvania. In 1902 Charles Nolan of the *Philadelphia North American* drew a year-long series in which he depicted Governor Pennypacker as a parrot, a mouthpiece for other forces. By 1903 the governor's patience was exhausted and he had an anticartoon bill introduced in the state legislature. "In England a century ago the [cartoonist] offender would have been drawn and quartered and his head stuck upon a pole," said the governor.

Cartoonist Walt McDougall came to the defense of his colleague by poking holes in Pennypacker's bill, which forbade using birds or animals to portray politicians. To McDougall's mind, the governor had failed to take account of a cartoonist's resourcefulness: "Every cartoonist has a Noah's ark of animals, bugs and such, but the vegetable field is untouched. What chances lie in the tomato, the string bean, the cucumber and the onion?" On the front page of the *North American,*

McDougall sketched the bill's proponents as a tree, a beer mug, and a turnip.

Similar attempts to pass anticartoon legislation were made in New York (1897), California (1899), Indiana (1913), and Alabama (1915). The laws produced laughter but not compliance and were eventually repealed.

As newspaper circulation has declined for the past fifty years, the death of the cartoon has been repeatedly predicted. Yet, as we will see, the craft has evolved and sustained many changes, and is very much alive. Today there exists an extraordinary, diverse range of styles and approaches to the medium of political satire, and any discussion must encompass not only editorial cartoonists but also comic strip artists and illustrators who sustain an ongoing political stance. We now set out to discover how successful cartoonists have been in tweaking the flaws in the democratic system and exposing hypocrisy wherever they find it. Let us meet these artists who, just for an instant, put a stick through the spokes of our spinning world and examine the issues and events they have drawn and quartered.

Paul Conrad, *Los Angeles Times*, September 30, 1982. ***In commenting on the eternal question of who is responsible for the United States' growing deficit, Paul Conrad put a contemporary spin on Nast's cartoon " Who Stole the People's Money?"***

THE BIRTH OF A NATIONAL IDENTITY: 1754 - 1865

POLITICAL CARTOONING is a symbolic art. The symbols are a shorthand, a convenience, not only for the artist but for the viewer as well. To alter the symbols, concluded cartoonist Don Hesse who drew for the *St. Louis Globe-Democrat,* "would be like changing the basic design of the American Flag, the Statue of Liberty, or Orphan Annie for that matter. Everyone has grown to know them all on sight. Since cartoonists strive for simplicity and for ideas unencumbered with labels, they use this cast of characters and eliminate the need for a program to tell the players one from the other." These symbols have become part of a cherished national heritage.

Benjamin Franklin (1706-90), May 9, 1754.

In 1754 Benjamin Franklin, who had already had a varied and illustrious career as a printer, inventor, and statesman, represented Pennsylvania at the Albany Congress, a convention called to deal with the problem of French and Indian forces threatening the colonies. He proposed a "Plan of Union" that would unite the colonies for defense purposes. In its support he drew a serpent divided into eight parts with the legend "Join or Die." The cartoon was based on a popular superstition that a snake that had been severed would come back to life if the pieces were put together before sunset. It appeared in the *Pennsylvania Gazette* of May 9, the first cartoon to be published in an American newspaper, and within a month had been reprinted by virtually every newspaper on the continent. The serpent was to have many lives. It was dusted off at the time of the Stamp Act crisis in 1765 and again when the colonies prepared to revolt in 1774.

Having the American revolutionaries depict their cause as a dissected snake was thought a good joke by one pro-British editor, James Rivington, who published this verse in his *New York Gazetteer.*

> *Ye sons of Sedition, how comes it to pass*
> *That America's typed by a snake-in-the-grass?*

Rivington was one of the first publishers to use illustrations in his newspaper. But his politics were not in keeping with the colonists, and

THE COUNTER MEDLEY

THE AMERICAN RATTLE SNAKE

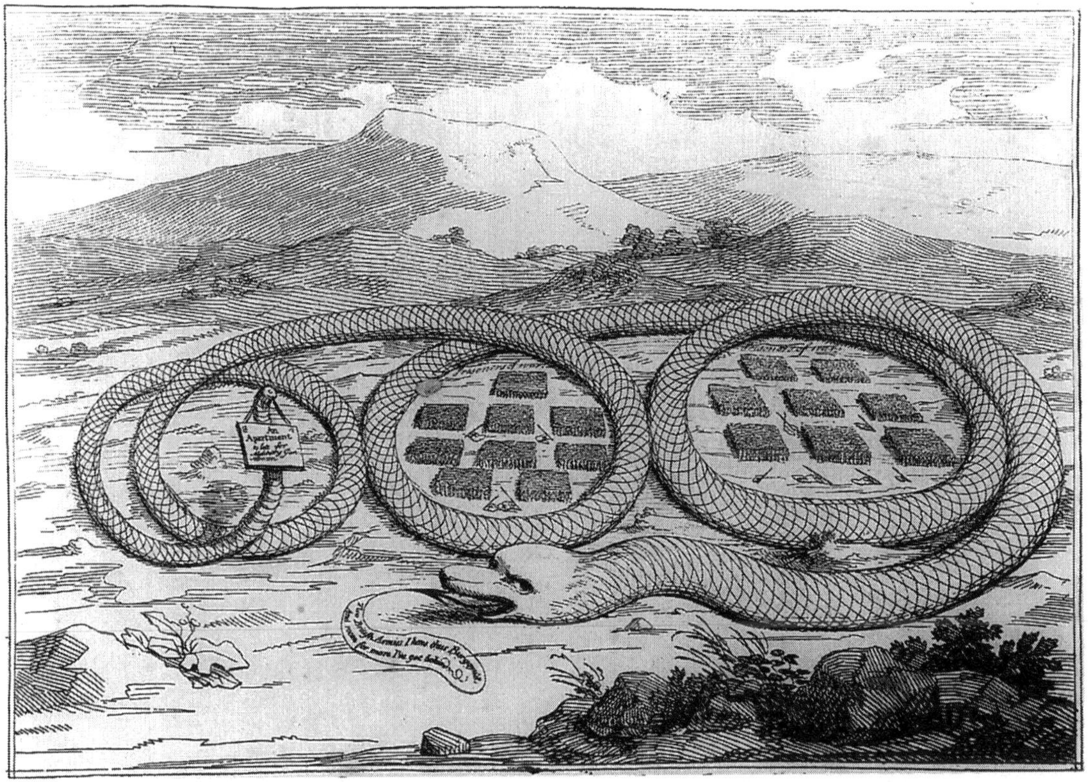

he was later hanged in effigy.

Yet the colonists would have the last laugh. For after General Cornwallis surrendered at Yorktown and the defeat of the English seemed assured, an engraving by English cartoonist James Gillray showed the rattlesnake encircling the British armies.

Franklin's snake as well as other symbols have been used and discarded over the years. The symbol "Salt River"—meaning political defeat—was created during the 1832 presidential election campaign between Henry Clay and Andrew Jackson. People living along the Mississippi River still tell the tale of how Clay hired a boat to take him to a political rally at a small river town. Unknown to Clay,

LEFT: Attributed to James Dove, 1764.
In this detail, the devil whispers in Benjamin Franklin's ear, "Thee shall be Agent Ben for all my realms." Franklin, the first American political cartoonist, was also the first public figure in America to have been ridiculed by cartoons.

RIGHT: James Gillray (1756-1815), April 12, 1782.

INKLINGS OF TRAVEL, UP SALT RIVER.

H. Bucholzer, 1848. ***All the presidential and vice-presidential candidates in the 1848 election are depicted here cruising up the Salt River into possible political oblivion.***

the boatman was a Jackson supporter and detoured his passenger into a tributary, the Salt River. Clay missed the rally and later lost the election. Cartoonists began depicting losing candidates (or those whom they wished to see lose) as falling into its waters.

Some symbols are invented to fill a void and have a provable paternity. Although the Democratic donkey and the Republican elephant are both often attributed to Thomas Nast, he is only entitled credit for the latter. There have been donkeys around as the symbol of the Democratic Party or of leading Democratic politicians since the days of Andrew Jackson. But the GOP elephant was born in a *Harper's Weekly* cartoon of November 7, 1874. (Nast, a good Republican, pictured the Democratic Party not as a donkey, but as a fox, and later as a tiger.) A number of attempts have been made to change the party symbols. The Democrats have been represented by a rooster in some southern states. The Republicans have used an eagle on the ballot in Oklahoma, and the Democrats have used the eagle in adjoining New Mexico. But the public has cast its ballot for the elephant and the donkey, even though they have lost whatever significance they might have originally had.

Many enduring symbols have simply evolved, with successive artists adding embellishments. Uncle Sam got his start during the War of 1812. Troops billeted in Troy, New York, near the Canadian border, received their meat provisions from Sam Wilson, a Hudson Valley supplier. Wilson was well liked by both the troops and the townspeople and was fondly referred to as Uncle Sam. The *U.S.* stamped on each crate of meat he delivered was said to be Wilson's personal stamp, not that of the United States of America.

THE REPUBLICAN NATIONAL COMMITTEE MEETS TO CONSIDER A NEW PARTY SYMBOL

ABOVE LEFT: Anonymous, 1837. *The first Democratic donkey.*

LEFT: Thomas Nast, *Harper's Weekly,* November 7, 1874. *The first Republican elephant.*

ABOVE: Arnold Roth, *Politicks Magazine*, 1977. *Over the years cartoonists have continued to have fun considering alternative party symbols.*

LEFT: Anonymous, 1776. ***Countless examples exist of the Indian as the symbol for the young colonies. This engraving was published on the eve of the Revolutionary War.*** **RIGHT: Amos Doolittle (1754-1832), October 21, 1813.** ***During the War of 1812, Americans delighted in Jonathan and turned him into a hero. Engraver Amos Doolittle showed Brother Jonathan forcing a British officer to drink a Yankee potion. Doolittle said his purpose was to "inspire our countrymen with confidence in themselves and eradicate any terrors that they may feel as respects the enemy they have to combat." By 1865, after nearly a century of service, Jonathan fell out of use.***

Before Uncle Sam made an appearance, the United States was represented by other figures, often simultaneously. An Indian—sometimes male, often female—was the earliest symbol of the young colonies. In 1755 British writers arrived at a more original appellation, "Yankee Doodle," a derisive term meant to categorize the rebels as country bumpkins. Shortly thereafter appeared the curious figure of "Brother Jonathan," another character created by British loyalists to poke fun at those who supported the American cause. British magazines often depicted Jonathan as the dupe of "John Bull," England's own national figure. "Columbia," a virtuous lady garbed in classical robes, was first used by American cartoonists to represent values and standards of the colonies and later the United States.

ABOVE: Anonymous, *Currier & Ives*, 1861. ***Instead of her classical garb, Columbia sports a dress style reminiscent of that worn during the Revolutionary War.***

RIGHT: Edwin Williams Clay (1799-1857), 1837. ***Uncle Sam is attended by doctor Andrew Jackson, apothecary Thomas Hart Benton (a supporter of Jackson's fiscal policies) who holds a large syringe, and a woman who bears a strong resemblance to Martin Van Buren. Sam holds a scroll that lists the amount of money lost in bank failures in New Orleans, New York, and Philadelphia. At far left, a bust of George Washington lies shattered on the ground.***

"Uncle Sam in Danger," Uncle Sam's first-known cartoon appearance in 1834, portrayed him as a sick man surrounded by quack doctors including President Andrew Jackson, Missouri Senator Thomas Hart Benton, and Vice President Martin Van Buren. The cartoon attacked Jackson's fight against a national bank and implied that President Jackson was "bleeding" the people's money from the Federal Treasury. Uncle Sam showed little resemblance to his modern-day counterpart; he was clean shaven, dressed in a nightcap, and wrapped in a blanket. A similar cartoon, "Uncle Sam Sick with La Grippe," penned three years later, borrowed the same setting and cast of characters to remark on the dire fiscal straits caused by

the bank failures of 1837. Uncle Sam now wears a cap labeled "Liberty" and a dressing gown patterned with stars and stripes.

Many of Uncle Sam's important characteristics were added by two London illustrators during the Civil War: Matt Morgan in *Fun* magazine and John Tenniel (best remembered as the illustrator of *Alice in Wonderland)* in *Punch* magazine. Under their clever manipulation Abraham Lincoln and Uncle Sam began to merge: clean-shaven Sam soon sported a beard, and Abe wore Sam's striped pants. Ironically, Uncle Sam's most recognizable characteristics were added to chastise Lincoln's attempts to hold the young nation together.

During the next sixty years, Sam made frequent appearances in cartoons. As his stature increased, he was often called upon to endorse candidates. Uncle Sam's role as the key anthropomorphic symbol representing America was confirmed in 1916 when James Montgomery Flagg redrew an earlier illustration to create a recruiting poster for World War I. The model for Uncle Sam was the artist himself. Four million copies of the poster were printed during World War I and 350,000 during World War II.

John Tenniel (1820-1914),
***Punch*,**
August 23, 1862.

Homer Davenport,
***Republican Campaign Poster*,**
1904.

While Uncle Sam's national profile grew, Columbia's waned and was eclipsed soon after the christening of Frederic Auguste Bartholdi's statue "Liberty Enlightening the World" in 1886. Although the nation's enthusiasm for the massive sculpture lagged—it would take ten years before public donations to build a base in New York's harbor were raised—the cartoonists' ardor for a new symbol ran high, and Liberty was immediately pressed into service. Uncle Sam and Liberty took on different roles: Sam represented the country; like Columbia, Liberty represented the country's values.

Uncle Sam remains an important symbol, although he is rarely given the reverence he once received. His use in modern cartoons shows the cynicism that pervades the profession today.

RIGHT: James Montgomery Flagg (1869-1956), United States Army Recruiting Service, 1917, adapted from a cover for *Leslie's Illustrated Weekly Newspaper*, July 6, 1916.

FAR RIGHT: Art Young (1860-1943), *Good Morning*, 1919.

BELOW: Tony Auth, *Philadelphia Inquirer*, October 4, 1974.

BELOW RIGHT: Jeff Danziger, *Christian Science Monitor*, December 30, 1987.

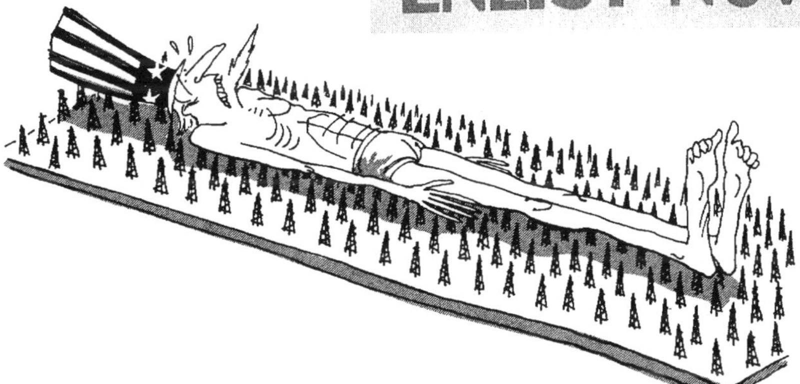

THE RISING OF THE USURPERS

"BACK HOME!"

Since her christening, Liberty has served as a spokesperson on myriad issues. Thomas Nast, one of the first to exploit the statue's potential, plastered Liberty with signs to demonstrate the growing power of trusts. Charles Werner was one of many to use Liberty to comment on the civil rights confrontations during the late 1950s and early 1960s. More recent cartoons have commented on immigration laws, government corruption, and industrial pollution.

LEFT: Thomas Nast, *Time*, July 27, 1889.

ABOVE: Vaughan Shoemaker (1902-91), *Chicago Daily News*, 1939.

RIGHT: Charles Werner (1909-97), *The Indianapolis Star*, 1950s.

"CAN'T GET GEORGIA OFF MY MIND!"

LEFT: Doug Marlette (1950-2007), ***Drawing Blood*****, 1980.**

BELOW: Signe Wilkinson, ***San Jose Mercury News*****, April 19, 1984.**

RIGHT: Mark Podual, 1970.

"OK. YOU HUDDLED MASSES. I KNOW YOU'RE IN HERE."

Jim Borgman, *Cincinnati Enquirer*, September 12, 1991. ***How important symbols are to cartoonists was clearly evident in this cartoon Jim Borgman drew after the fall of the Soviet Union. Having grown used to the bear and the hammer and sickle, cartoonists have yet to find suitable replacements.***

Just as cartoonists have always had some character to represent the American nation and its values, so, too, has there always been a character to represent the American people. In the 1830s and 1840s he was called Major Jack Downing after a fictional Yankee peddler. In most cartoons Downing was down-home, even crass, but showed good common sense, a trait that remains important in defining the American character. At the end of the nineteenth century, Frederick Opper drew a little man and labeled him "The Common People." He also would be known as "John Public," and around 1930 Vaughn Shoemaker, then of the *Chicago Daily News,* gave him a middle initial: John Q. Public.

Today, Uncle Sam and the Statue of Liberty maintain their vigilance at drawing boards across America. Other symbols such as "Mr. Atom," created by *Washington Post* cartoonist Herbert Block in 1947 to show the daunting threat of atomic war, served brief but important moments in the nation's visual vocabulary. Many of today's cartoonists avoid

Frederick Opper (1857-1937), *The Arena*, 1905.

using symbols, calling them a throwback to earlier days when the audience was not as sophisticated, but as cartoonist Rollin Kirby once remarked about Uncle Sam, "It would be difficult to manage a daily cartoon without him."

Long before the tradition of political satire established itself in the young United States of America, European artists had been producing diversified and devastating caricatures to speak out against perceived injustices. In England, the raw, robust artistry of William Hogarth helped turn the eighteenth century into "the century of caricature." But James Gillray, the first master draftsman to devote himself to the regular production of political satires, would have a far more profound impact on the emerging American cartoonists.

Even the word "cartoon" is part of America's debt to its mother country. Gillray's work was known as "caricature." At the time, "cartoon" meant no more than the preliminary sketch for a fresco or painting. But when in July 1843 the British government held an exhibition of paintings commissioned to beautify the houses of Parliament, the humor magazine *Punch,* feeling that there were better uses for the money, published a cartoon of a ragged crowd inspecting the show. And this "Cartoon No. I," as the John Leech drawing was titled, made an unexpected contribution to the English language.

LEFT: James Gillray (1756-1815), February 26, 1805. RIGHT: Draper Hill (1935-2009), *Detroit News*, October 6, 1976. *Cartoonist Draper Hill borrowed from Gillray to suggest the scope of an upcoming presidential campaign debate between Gerald Ford and Jimmy Carter.*

Yet it was in France that the incendiary power of the cartoon was realized under the masterful supervision of Charles Philipon, who published the magazine *La Caricature* and a daily newspaper, *Le Charivari* (which in 1841 inspired the founding *of Punch,* subtitled "The London Charivari"). Philipon hired Honoré Daumier, Gustave Doré, and other outstanding artists. Their drawings became one of the more effective weapons in their growing struggle for journalistic independence against the King Louis Philippe.

In 1831, as censorship increased, Philipon invented "la poire," or pear, to symbolize the king. *(La poire* means "fathead" in French slang.) The symbol was used by all of Philipon's artists and became the most famous and effective political emblem of its time. Cartoon after cartoon made the pear-shaped ruler an object of ridicule to his subjects. For this brilliant satire Philipon was put on trial, and in his own defense drew a large Burgundy pear, which he converted in a few strokes to a likeness of the king. "Can I help it if His Majesty's face is like a pear?" he asked. Philipon was ordered not to draw the king as a pear again. It did not prevent him, however, from setting the type of an article rendering the court's judgment in the shape of the forbidden fruit.

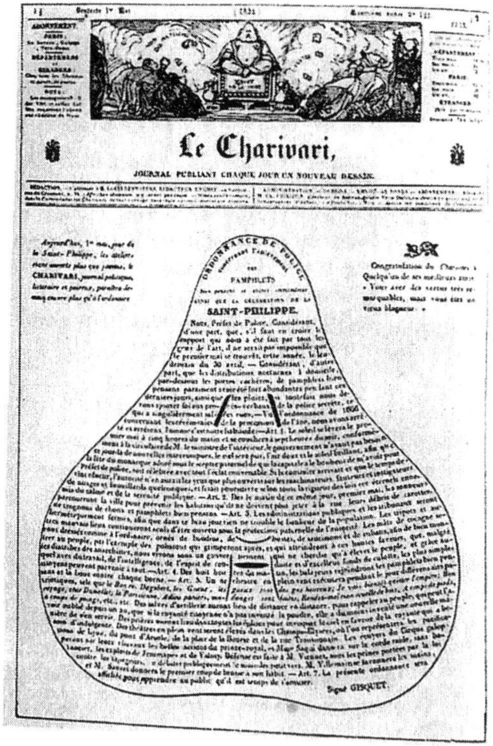

LEFT: Charles Philipon (1800-62), *Le Charivari*, January 17, 1831.
RIGHT: Charles Philipon, *Le Charivari*, May 1, 1835.

While European cartoonists made monarchs the subject of their satire, their American counterparts had the fledgling office of the presidency to attack. George Washington would be the first but not the last president to discover that the cartooning fraternity respected neither rank nor previous achievement. Shortly after Washington's inauguration in 1789, fellow Revolutionary officer John Armstrong wrote General Gates from New York: "All the world here are busy in collecting

THE TIMES, A POLITICAL PORTRAIT

Anonymous, 1795. ***During his second term as the first U.S. president, Washington issued a proclamation declaring neutrality in the war between England and France. It was a strong but not necessarily popular decision. Congress felt he had usurped its power. In this sympathetic Federalist portrait, Washington is guarded by soldiers as "French Cannibals" are turned back from the American shore. The man trying to halt the "wheels of government" is Thomas Jefferson. Benjamin Franklin Bache, grandson of the famous patriot, is shown being trampled by the passing cavalcade while, in the foreground, his newspaper, Aurora, which criticized the president's decision, gets equally ignominious treatment.***

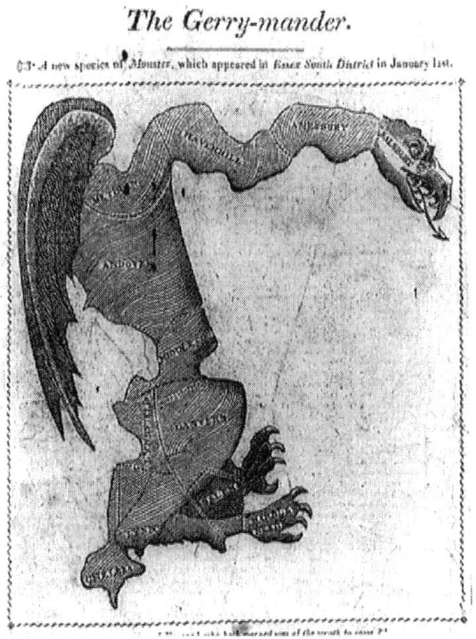

Elkanah Tisdale (1771-1834), *Boston Gazette*, March 26, 1812. *Possibly the best—certainly the most famous—of the early-nineteenth-century cartoons was drawn by Elkanah Tisdale. When the Democratic majority arbitrarily realigned the voting district of Essex County to ensure Massachusetts Gov. Elbridge Gerry's reelection, Tisdale invented a new political monster and aptly dubbed it "Gerry-mander."*

flowers and sweets of every kind to amuse and delight the President. Yet in the midst of this admiration there are skeptics who doubt its propriety, and wits who amuse themselves at its extravagance. The first will grumble and the last will laugh, and the President should be prepared to meet the attacks of both with firmness and good nature. A caricature has already appeared, called 'The Entry,' full of very disloyal and profane allusions."

No copy of this print exists, but it is known to have shown Washington riding on a donkey led by his aide, David Humphreys. The accompanying couplet read:

The glorious time has come to pass
When David shall conduct an ass.

Washington was treated gently compared to Thomas Jefferson. Today it is almost impossible to find a pro-Jefferson cartoon. A typical example shows the third president kneeling at the "Altar of Gallic Despotism," about to throw the Constitution into the flames. Jefferson had been the American colony's first representative to France, and was known to have admired the country, its people, and its wine.

During the colonial period and the early years of the Republic, the appearance of a political cartoon in America was an event of considerable rarity. There are only seventy-eight known political caricatures issued as broadsides—small handouts printed on individual sheets of paper—before 1828. Cartoons in newspapers and magazines appeared even less frequently. Newsprint was extremely expensive and so scarce that at times readers were requested to save rags for the paper mills. Publishers had little means to pay for cartoons that had to be laboriously engraved on copper or cut into wood. Cartoons in publications were used primarily to illustrate major events. It was not unknown for the same drawing to be used many times to illustrate different events. Even as late as the Civil War it was possible to find a Confederate magazine using an unflattering illustration to depict Abraham Lincoln and the next month using the same illustration to depict abolitionist Horace Greeley.

For political cartoons to have mass readership in the United States required two developments: a process that could cut the cost of production and a subject colorful enough to inspire broad interest and controversy. The election year of 1828 produced both lithography and Andrew Jackson. To some, Jackson

THE PROVIDENTIAL DETECTION

Anonymous, 1797. ***This cartoon comments on the outcome of the 1796 presidential election in which John Adams defeated Thomas Jefferson. The United States, represented by the eagle under the watchful eye of Providence, has triumphed over Jefferson and his distinctly non-Federalist ideas, thus saving the Constitution.***

RICHARD III.

David Claypoole Johnston (1799-1865). ***Jackson's military career came back to haunt him when he ran for president in 1828. The Hero of New Orleans had been a demanding and often ruthless commander, and in 1814 had ordered four soldiers shot for desertion. In this finely detailed engraving, Jackson's face and epaulets are crafted from the dead bodies of his military career.***

Anonymous, 1837. *Jackson's decentralization of the National Bank brought disasterous results and led to the economic crisis of 1837. State banks issued bills that frequently had no capital behind them. "Shin plaster" was the name given to small-denomination notes that were elaborately decorated but worthless. In this cartoon the artist creates his own currency to show his views: Jackson rushes toward an inevitable fall over the cliff, while Martin Van Buren, Jackson's successor, takes a more conservative path toward fiscal responsibility.*

was a savior, the common man's friend, a warrior who led them in battle against the British at the Battle of New Orleans in 1812 and against privileged interests in their own country; to others he was a tyrant.

Jackson's two terms in office would be predicated on the belief that a large chasm separated the haves and the have-nots. In his second term he refused to recharter the United States Bank, calling it a monopoly that was designed to make "rich men richer ... by act of congress." The recharter question was the first issue to become the subject of numerous cartoons covered from many viewpoints. The argument divided along party lines.

Lithography, a process of drawing directly on a stone that was much less time-consuming than engraving, soon gave America its first affordable art. The firm of Currier & Ives, established in 1835, "was the first to offer for sale to the American people, at low prices, a wider variety of colored and effectively drawn pictures that were always easy to appreciate and the subject matter of which was always

KING ANDREW THE FIRST.

APRÈS MOI LE DELUGE

LEFT: Anonymous, 1832. RIGHT: Edward Sorel, *Washington Post Book World*, 1973. *Using the figure of a king, czar or emperor as a symbol for a president who had risen too far above his electorate became a staple for American cartoonists. Jackson's opponents made effective use of this imagery during his reelection campaign in 1832. Sorel's commentary on Richard Nixon at the time of the Watergate hearings is equally telling.*

Storefront of Currier & Ives, New York City, circa 1865.

Currier & Ives political prints chronicle the presidential elections from 1836 to 1876 and the issues the candidates debated. Company policy was business above politics as Mr. Currier and Mr. Ives turned out cartoons for all sides at the same time. Moreover, in periods when feelings ran high, artistic pride gave way to commercial prudence, and the firm left its name off the prints or signed them with the pseudonym Peter Smith. When Abraham Lincoln, the Republican candidate in 1860, opposed two candidates from a fractured Democratic Party as well as another independent party candidate, the print shop supplied campaign material for every side, all drawn by the same skilled hands. Prints were sold to party headquarters at bulk rates, although they could also be purchased individually at

Louis Maurer (1832-1932), *Currier & Ives*, 1860.

popular and always American," wrote Harry T. Peters, who chronicled the firm's long life. They produced more than ten million prints on nearly 7,000 different subjects—great fires, wildlife, railroads, landscapes, society scenes, Indians, sporting events, and more than eighty political cartoons. Interested buyers gathered daily at their display window in New York City to see the newest editions.

Louis Maurer, Currier & Ives, 1860. ***Lincoln's fence rail—the symbol of his humble beginnings—is present in nearly every cartoon about Lincoln during the 1860 campaign. Special interest groups appear to have had as much influence in politics then as they do today. Lincoln's supporters in this cartoon include a suffragist, a Mormon, a free-love advocate, and a socialist, among others.***

PROGRESSIVE DEMOCRACY—PROSPECT OF A SMASH UP.

Louis Maurer, Currier & Ives, 1860. ***In this comment on the 1860 split in the Democratic Party (with the Tammany Indian pictured as holding the reins of the northern ticket), the artist hangs human heads in front of animal ears, a technique associated with an earlier style of cartooning rarely seen in this period. The face of Lincoln in all the 1860 Currier & Ives cartoons was taken from a Mathew Brady photograph. Later, when Lincoln began to grow a beard, the lithographer's stones were given the appropriate touch-up.*** **NEAR RIGHT: John C. Breckinridge. FAR RIGHT: Joseph Lane.** ***The portraits in Maurer's lithograph were obviously copied from these photographs.***

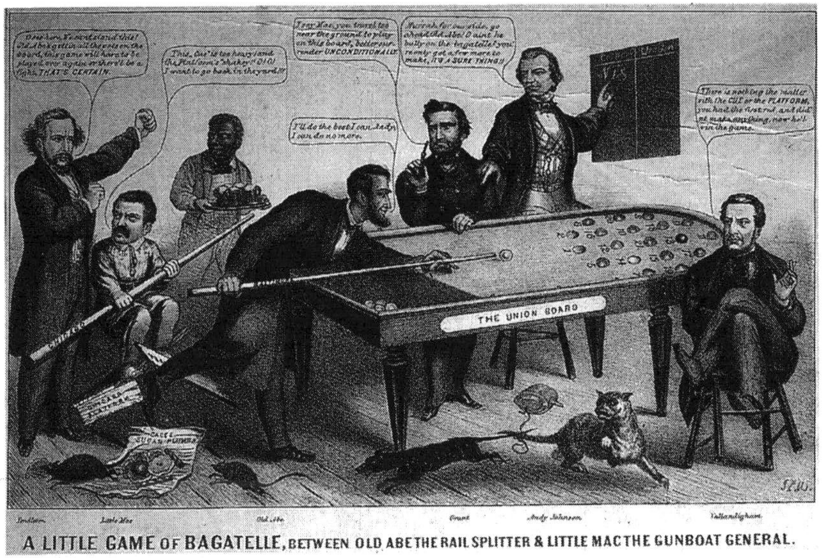

LEFT: Anonymous, *Currier & Ives*, 1864. RIGHT: Louis Maurer, *Currier & Ives*, 1860. *Using sports motifs was as popular in the nineteenth century as now. Any presidential election was sure to be presented as a horse or foot race, a boxing match, a game of brag (an early version of poker), pool, or bagatelle, a cockfight, hunting, fishing, a bull fight, or (by 1860) a baseball game.*

prices ranging from five to twenty-five cents.

Although the Currier & Ives cartoons sometimes displayed a good sense of composition, the figures were stiff and spiritless. Huge, balloonlike loops of text usually wafted from their mouths, a method of storytelling by then abandoned in Europe, which reminded writers Arthur Maurice and Frederic Cooper, respectively, of "a soap-bubble party on a large scale" and "the cowboys of a Wild West show, all engaged in a vain attempt to lasso and pull in their own Idle words."

Whatever humor can be found in these political lithographs came from the juxtaposition—the incongruous and ridiculous situations in which the artists placed these men—rather than from any exaggeration or distortion of the subjects' features. The portraiture of the Currier & Ives artists was so exact that it is clear the engravers worked directly from daguerreotypes or photographs.

Pictorially and textually, prints of the 1800s relied heavily on the pun, a practice, apparently, that was not limited to cartoonists. A *Vanity Fair* author in 1860, noting the reliance of so many early American comics on this form of humor, wrote: "I would restrict the allowance of a punster in good health to 80 or 90 a day, certainly not more than a hundred. I frequently make 6 or 700 before dinner, but

FRANK LESLIE'S ILLUSTRATED NEWSPAPER

NEW YORK, FEBRUARY 1, 1862.

GUARD-HOUSE NEAR LANGLEY, VA.

COL. MURPHY'S REGIMENT OF PONTONIERS

February 1, 1862. ***During the Civil War, Leslie's cover usually depicted a battlefield scene. Leslie's artists referred to photographs and illustrations sent from the front, often copying directly from these visuals to produce each week's engravings. The photoengraving process that enabled newspapers to use the photographs themselves would first be used in 1880 by the*** **New York Daily Graphic,** ***but it wasn't until 1897 that the method was perfected for regular use.***

then everybody has not my constitution."

The gathering and disseminating of news changed rapidly in the 1800s. The invention of the telegraph in 1844 made news up to date. The Civil War was the first long-run news event in the history of American journalism, and reporters collided with generals on the battlefield. Wives and sweethearts eagerly awaited the reports from the front lines.

One man in particular would dramatically visualize the war for those on the homefront. Henry Carter, born in Ipswich, England, pioneered illustrated journalism in America under the name Frank Leslie. Trained as an engraver, Leslie speeded up the process of pictorial reporting by an ingenious, yet simple, device. When covering a fast-breaking event, he was able to get into print sooner than his competitors by cutting his illustrations into sections and distributing parts among a number of engravers. In some illustrations thirty-two separate sections were pieced together. His most famous journal, *Frank Leslie's Illustrated Newspaper* (later called *Frank Leslie's Illustrated Weekly*), made its debut in late 1855 and sold for ten cents a copy. Although the successful meshing of magazine publishing and political cartoons would not occur until the close of the

Civil War, Frank Leslie set the stage, both by first employing the artists who would usher in the golden age of American cartooning, and by conditioning the country to a new style of lively journalism.

Frank Bellew was one of Leslie's first cartoonists. "Frank Bellew's pencil is extraordinary," commented Charles Dickens's London magazine, *All the Year Round.* "He probably originated more, of a purely comic nature, than all the rest of his artistic brethren put together." Incredibly prolific, Bellew's artwork appeared regularly in *Leslie's Illustrated Newspaper* and other publications that tried to emulate London's *Punch,* such as *Lantern, Yankee Notions, Momus, Reveille, Picayune, Vanity Fair,* the *Harper's* magazines, *Phuniest of Phun* (which he edited), *Punchinello, Wild Oats, New York Daily Graphic,* and *Scribner's.* Most never made a first anniversary; some never saw a second issue.

Bellew and other cartoonists delighted in the comic aspects provided by Abraham Lincoln's elongated ungainly frame, his homely features, even his habit of spicing his speeches with amusing stories. What Lincoln thought of the cartoonists is unknown. But he must have studied their work, for a cartoon that pictured him as the high-wire artist Blondin crossing Niagara Falls suggested a metaphor that Lincoln was to use in an important meeting with a committee of senators. It has also been said that he was deeply hurt by a drawing of himself as two-faced, in which his denial of presidential ambitions in 1858 is contrasted with his quest for the nomination two years later. (The cartoon is so innocuous, however, that it is difficult to believe it could sting a seasoned politician.)

Nor did the president have much cause to fear the pencil of Southern artists. The few humor magazines put out in the Confederate States—*Southern Illustrated News* (Richmond), *Southern Punch* (Richmond), and *Bugle Horn of Liberty* (Griffin, Georgia)—were pathetic documents. The most powerful cartooning from the Southern standpoint was done by German-born Adalbert J. Volck, who set up shop as a dentist in Baltimore's German American community in 1851. Baltimore was a port city filled with slave auctions, tobacco warehouses, and docks choked with cargo bound for the South. It had become a hotbed for secessionist sympathy by 1861. According to Kendall B. Mattern Jr., who studied Volck's work, the dentist volunteered his services to the Southern cause, shepherding those who

LONG ABRAHAM LINCOLN, A LITTLE LONGER

LEFT:
Frank Bellow (1828-88), *Harper's Weekly,* November 26, 1884.

BELOW:
Caricature of Frank Bellow, Livingston Hopkins (1846-1927), *Wild Oats.* November 12, 1847.

Adalbert Volck (1828-1912), *Sketches of the Civil War in North America, 1862. Volk shows his intense hatred of the North in this cartoon in which a white man is sacrificed on the altar of "Negro Worship." As propaganda for the Confederacy, Volck's work had little effect. Few saw his etchings until after the war. Yet arguably this dentist's delicate lines and scathing compositions were the finest drawings produced during the Civil War.*

ABOVE: Anonymous, *Southern Illustrated News*, February 28, 1863. *Lincoln's difficulty in finding a general provided the inspiration for one of the rare hits in a Confederate journal.*

Thomas Nast, *Harper's Weekly*, September 3, 1864, *Nast's indictment of those who sought a compromise to end the war was reproduced by the millions as a Republican campaign document and was credited by many as insuring the reelection of Lincoln.*

wanted to join the Confederate forces across the Potomac River into Virginia and housing both Confederate soldiers and Southern sympathizers under his roof. Then Volck, who had no art training, turned to etching as a further means of helping the Confederacy.

Dentist by day, engraver by night, over the next four years Volck would secretly produce a collection of etchings under the title *Sketches of the Civil War in North America,* in which he contrasted the noble struggle of the South against the barbarism of the North.

On the Union side, another German immigrant, Thomas Nast, was hired by *Harper's Weekly.* Harper Brothers had started a monthly magazine in 1850 designed to avoid political controversy, serialize English novels, and promote the firm's books. Seven years later, after Frank Leslie had demonstrated that there was a large market for an illustrated weekly, the Harpers entered the field. Their weekly magazine became "the fighting arm" of the publishing house.

Hired to render illustrations from sketches that came in from artists on the battlefields, Nast, who worked in Harper's New York offices, gradually sought compositions that went beyond mere description of events to the deeper meaning of the Civil War. One of these "emblematic" messages, which appeared shortly after the Democratic National Convention in 1864 adopted a peace platform, was entitled "Compromise with the South." According to an 1876 profile of Nast, "Seldom has an artist achieved fame as suddenly as Nast did by this single effort."

Vanity Fair was the third important magazine to emerge during the war, an upscale ripoff of the enormously popular London *Vanity Fair.* The magazine initially opposed the unknown country lawyer from Illinois, but after Lincoln's election, gave him qualified support. It was consistent in its antiabolitionist stand, however. The magazine considered the Negro inferior and believed that freeing the slaves would bring turmoil. H. L. Stephens, one of the magazine's founders and its most prominent artist, presented that point of view in "What Will He Do with Them?" The artist set up the president's dilemma by portraying Lincoln as a peddler carrying cages full of blackbirds and pondering, "Darn, these blackbirds. If nobody won't buy them, I'll have to open the cages and let them fly." Stephens greeted the Emancipation Proclamation with a cartoon of a freed black man heading for his new home. "Yah! Dis chile's on de move to his new sutumvation. Wonder what sort of psum new Massa's gwine be!" *Vanity Fair* folded before the war's end.

Lincoln's handling of the war came under severe attack from the British press. The *London Times* remarked more in joy than in sorrow on how short-lived the union of the American states had been, and how there were men still alive who had

LEFT: H. L. Stephens (1824-82), *Vanity Fair*, between September 6, 1862 and July 4, 1863.

RIGHT: Matt Morgan (1828-90), *Fun*, July 18, 1863.

witnessed the birth of what was now a dying nation. British cartoonists, reflecting their government's position, supplied some of the crudest barbs. Lincoln's chief detractors from the mother country were John Tenniel of *Punch* and Matt Morgan of *Fun.*

Punch's cartoons were always collectively arrived at during Wednesday night editorial dinners. When Lincoln was assassinated, *Punch* paid the slain leader an eloquent tribute: the obituary cartoon was a Tenniel composition showing Britannia laying a wreath on Lincoln's bier. Printed under the drawing was an eleven-stanza poem by Tom Taylor, *Punch's* editor, in which the magazine reproached itself for its attitude toward Lincoln. This effort, however, was not without opposition. Shirley Brooks, a future *Punch* editor, wrote in his diary: "Dined Punch. All there. Let out my views against some verses on Lincoln in which T. T. had not only made P. eat humble pie, but swallow dish and all."

In 1905 Adalbert Volck gave his Civil War portfolio to the Library of Congress. In a letter that accompanied the bequest he wrote, "I feel the greatest regret ever to have aimed ridicule at that great and good Lincoln."

John Tenniel, *Punch*, May 6, 1865. Two stanzas from Tom Taylor's poem:

You lay a wreath on murdered Lincoln's bier,
You, who with mocking pencil wont to trace,
Broad for the self-complacent British sneer,
His length of shambling limb, his furrowed face.

Yes, he had lived to shame me from my sneer,
To lame my pencil, and confute my pen—
To make me own this hind of princes peer,
This Rail-splitter a true born king of men.

THE RISE OF THE AMERICAN CARTOON: 1865 - 1896

IN THE YEARS FOLLOWING the Civil War, America was engulfed by great tides of immigration, massive industrialization, and widespread political corruption. An invigorated press would evolve to chronicle these developments, using elaborate illustrations and cartoons to reinforce the text. During the next three decades the craft of cartooning would be honed and elevated to the plateau of art. Two German immigrants, Thomas Nast and Joseph Keppler, would set the standards for the fledgling craft—standards of excellence that are still the hallmark of the profession.

Printing House Square, New York City, circa 1865. ***New York City was the hub for publishing in the United States, and Printing House Square was at its center. The offices of many newspapers, including the* New York World, New York Sun, New York Times, *and* New York Tribune, *faced onto the square. Most of these buildings would be torn down to make way for the Brooklyn Bridge. The original* New York Times *building, however, remains at the corner of Spruce and Nassau Streets.***

The popularity of illustrated news magazines such as *Leslie's Illustrated* and *Harper's Weekly* had continued to grow since the end of the war. One enthusiastic *Leslie's* reader wrote: "The illustrated papers of the country supply us with a response to our curiosity, and so thoroughly that the great men and great places of the world are almost as familiar to us today as our own home and neighbors. The influence of the newspapers in politics is nowadays so well acknowledged that every party must have its organs, or it is impossible for it to hope for success."

Thomas Nast was born in 1840 in Landau, Germany, the son of a Bavarian soldier. He was six when he arrived in New York; sixteen when he became a staff artist on *Frank Leslie's Illustrated Newspaper;* twenty-four when, during the Civil War, President Lincoln said of him, "Thomas Nast has been our best recruiting sergeant."

His work for *Harper's Weekly* during the war had made both the artist and the magazine famous. Readership reached across the American plains to California. The magazine would become the greatest political power in postbellum publishing because of the collaboration of Nast and editor George William

LEFT: A.R. Waud (1828-91), *Harper's Weekly*, November 16, 1867.

ABOVE: Frank Bellew, *Fifth Avenue Journal*, 1872. *Frank Bellew captures the animosity between Thomas Nast and his editor George William Curtis, which was kept in check by the publisher Fletcher Harper. After Harper's death, however, the differences between the two men became irreconcilable.*

THE "BRAINS"

THAT ACHIEVED THE TAMMANY VICTORY AT THE ROCHESTER DEMOCRATIC CONVENTION.

Thomas Nast, *Harper's Weekly*, October 21, 1871. ***In this single figure, the artist created the perfect cartoon: the idea is humorous; the drawing is well executed; the message is to the point; the symbolism is clear but not (yet) a cliché. In addition to Tweed's obesity, by this stage in the campaign Nast is able to identify the Boss merely by his $15,500 diamond stickpin. A hint of Tweed's facial features is even present in the $.***

RIGHT: Thomas Nast, *Harper's Weekly*, November 25, 1871. ***Tweed actually won reelection, but the Tammany Ring was crippled by Nast's attack and would never regain its previous power.***

"WHAT ARE YOU LAUGHING AT? TO THE VICTOR BELONG THE SPOILS."

Curtis; yet the fiery cartoonist and the Puritan editor formed an uneasy alliance. Nast once said that when Curtis "attacks a man with his pen it seems as if he were apologizing for the act. I try to hit the enemy between the eyes and knock him down." Curtis felt there was something ungentlemanly about a political cartoon. It was so stark, so final, so incapable of suggesting "but on the other hand...." Nast would not be the last cartoonist to feel that his own voice was compromised by an editor.

Nast's fame was to rest mainly on some fifty drawings he did in 1871 when, in tandem with the *New York Times, Harper's Weekly* focused the nation's attention on the rampant corruption surrounding Tammany Hall, the Democratic Party machine controlling New York politics, particularly the excesses revealed in building the new county courthouse. Both the *New York Times* and *Harper's Weekly* were Republican publications and openly hostile toward the Democrats' prolonged control of the city. Nast's bold designs and strong gift for caricature eventually centered on William M. "Boss" Tweed as the ringleader. As journalism scholar Thomas Leonard comments, "Nast transformed Tweed into a menace. He created ways to picture a corrupt city. It was a far cry from anything that had been accomplished by journalists before him." Nast's influence on public opinion was enormous.

On July 21, 1871, *New York Times* readers opened their newspapers to pages that looked like balance sheets: New York County ledger books, documenting fraud. More than half a million copies of the "Secret Accounts" were grabbed up at newsstands. The excesses were mind-numbing: for nine months of labor of one plasterer, Andrew Garvey, the amount of $2,870,464.83; a bill from Messrs Ingersoll and Co. for furniture and fittings for $5,663,646.83; a bill from Keyser and Co. for plumbing for $1,231,817.76. In the three months before the November election, Nast produced as many Tammany cartoons as he had in the previous three years. With each new issue of *Harper's Weekly* the city's newsdealers found eager crowds waiting to see the cartoons. In one two-week period, 125,000 readers were added.

Where earlier cartoons rarely ventured beyond recognizable portraits, Nast used caricature to drive home his point. The result was brilliant and compelling: William M. Tweed became the very symbol of evil. "Whatever transgression the real Tweed did or did not commit, it was Nast's Tweed the American public came to loathe," writes historian Roger Fischer. (Nast's gift was also used to portray good: his annual drawings of Santa Claus refined and standardized the image of the "jolly old elf" presented in the Clement C. Moore poem "A Visit from St. Nicholas.")

Today Thomas Nast is remembered as a crusader, the invincible artist exposing injustice with the stroke of a pen, but this perception is not completely accurate. The brilliance of his penmanship will never be doubted, yet the nobility of the causes he championed must be questioned. Nast remained steadfast in his loyalty to the Ulysses S. Grant administration

Thomas Nast, *Harper's Weekly*, November 25, 1871. *Sitting atop the press is our hero, Tom Nast, madly sketching. That the audience would be so familiar with the cartoonist's features that no identification was necessary shows the extent of Nast's celebrity.*

SOMETHING THAT DID BLOW OVER—NOVEMBER 7, 1871.

Thomas Nast, *Harper's Weekly*, November 25, 1871. *After the election Nast pictures Mayor Hall still clinging to the remains of the building since no vote had been taken on his office. Hall was considered the least culpable of the Tweed Ring. He ended his days writing for comic magazines.*

COLUMBIA—"HANDS OFF GENTLEMEN! AMERICA MEANS FAIR PLAY FOR ALL MEN."

LEFT: Thomas Nast, *Harper's Weekly*, March 17, 1867. RIGHT: Thomas Nast, *Harper's Weekly*, February 18, 1871. *Perhaps because the Chinese "problem" was in California, 3,000 miles away, Nast usually supported better treatment of the Chinese in his cartoons.*

even when the full story of its corruption and incompetence was known. In accordance with the Republican Party, Nast supported the rights of the newly freed slave and even took the side of the persecuted Chinese in the West, but his own bigotry emerged in hostile characterizations of the Irish, particularly Irish Catholics. In the same 1871 issues of *Harper's* in which he pulled the rug out from under the Tammany Gang, Nast created vicious caricatures and tableaux attacking the Irish upon whom Tammany Hall relied for their votes.

Nonetheless, Nast's cartoons were a major circulation-builder for *Harper's Weekly.* The fight with Tweed tripled the magazine s readership, but in later years Nast continually battled Curtis for editorial autonomy. Rather then draw a cartoon in support of a position with which he disagreed, he stood by his convictions and refused to draw. In doing so Richard West notes, "He became the first journalist to make an issue of professional integrity, a concept that today is taken largely for granted.

OUR ARTIST'S OCCUPATION GONE

ABOVE: Thomas Nast, *Harper's Weekly*, November 11, 1872. *Nast pictures himself as the taciturn, moody individual he probably was. With Tammany Hall in ruins and Grant having won a second term in office, the artist suggests that now that the two causes he has championed have been successful, he has put himself out of a job.*

ABOVE RIGHT: Joseph Keppler, *Puck*, August 10, 1881. *Keppler's playfulness is reflected in this self-caricature. As he sleeps, some of the politicians Keppler has depicted repaint his images of them. The competition between Nast and Keppler must have been fierce. Although they worked in the same town and shared a common cultural heritage, there is no record of the two artists ever meeting.*

A MID-SUMMER DAY'S DREAM

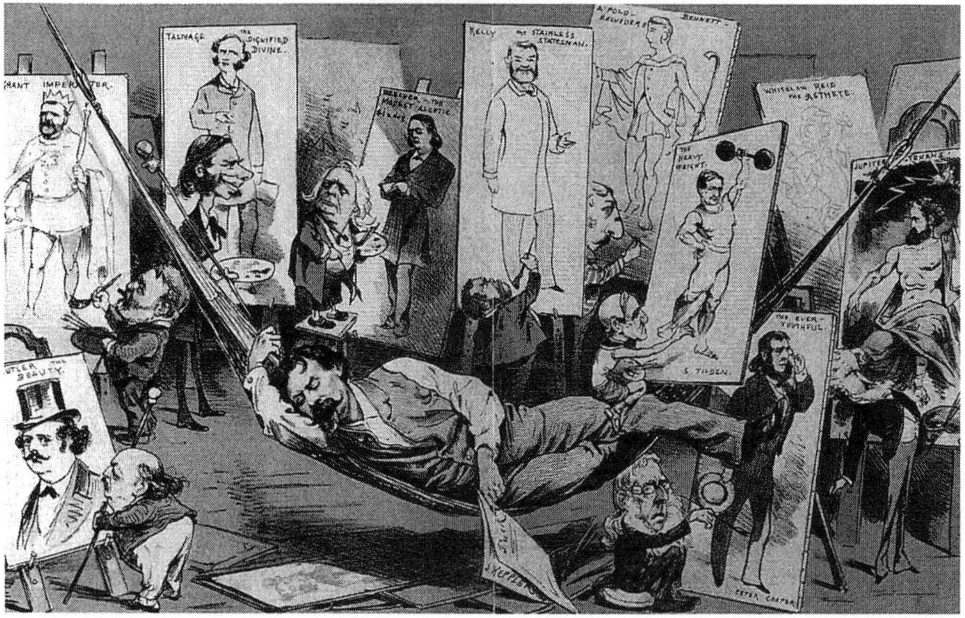

But in Nast's day, the idea was ridiculed." Gradually Nast lost his audience and support. In 1887 he left the magazine. "In quitting *Harper's Weekly*," said a newspaper editor at the time, "Nast lost his forum; in losing him, *Harper's Weekly* lost its political influence." The magazine would never again be so powerful, although the cartoonist's departure was not the sole reason for its decline. In 1890 Nast established his own magazine, *Nast's Weekly*. It failed after five months, and he began to travel the country, often leaving home for months at a time to support his family by lecturing with chalkboard, wit, and charm.

As Nast's fortunes waned, a new cartoonist captured the fancy of the American public. His work was less cumbersome than Nast's, gayer and more graceful; hardly likely to incite riot, though still capable of drawing blood. Joseph Keppler's weapon was the rapier, not the broadsword. The son of a Viennese baker (his earliest artistry appeared as the ornamentation on his father's cakes), Keppler's principal occupation was that of actor when he arrived in St. Louis in 1867 at the age of twenty-nine. St. Louis, by then the United States' third-largest city, had a large and thriving German American community and published four daily German-language newspapers. After a fling on the American stage and the founding of two short-lived humor magazines, in 1872 Keppler left St. Louis for New York and joined Frank Leslie's stable of artists. Four years later he took a second stab at publishing. Together with Adolph Schwarzmann, Keppler brought out a German-language weekly called *Puck,* which took its name from the elfin character in Shakespeare's *Midsummer Night's Dream.* An English edition followed the next year.

Puck was different. Where all previous American humor magazines had been modeled on London's *Punch,* Keppler brought a totally new perspective to his journal of fun and satire. Its covers sported a different cartoon each week instead of one traditional design. Emblazoned on each cover was the magazine's trademark, Puck, drawn in the likeness of Keppler's daughter. Most importantly, *Puck's* centerfold and front and back covers were in color.

There was also something a bit exotic about the new magazine, perhaps an air of Viennese gaiety that Keppler and his imported artists, F. Graetz and Karl Edler von Stur, brought to their creations. (Graetz spoke no

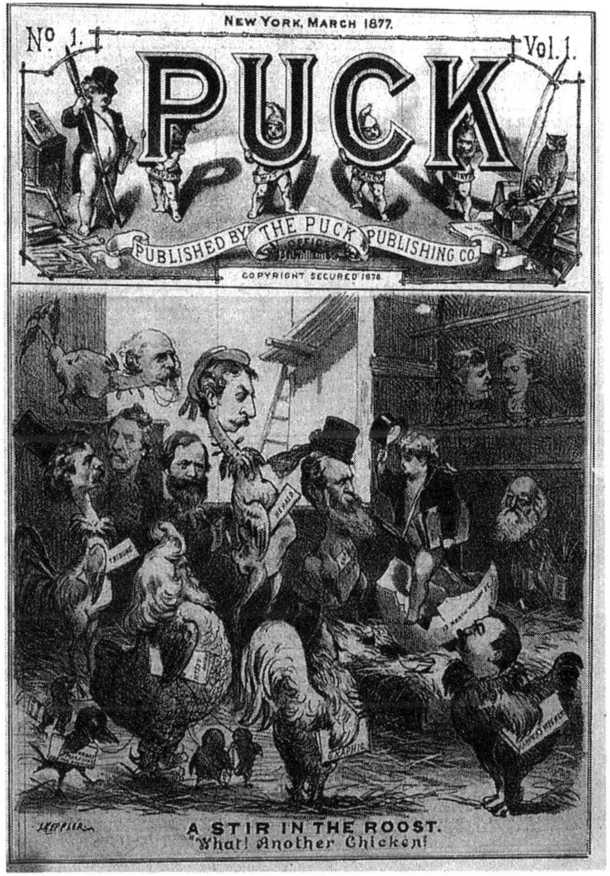

ABOVE: *The Puck figure was a popular trademark. When Keppler built a new building in 1886, statues of the whimsical Puck looked down from two corners. The building on Houston Street in lower Manhattan in now a registered national landmark.*

LEFT: Joseph Keppler, *Puck, (Inaugural Issue)* March 14, 1877. *Among the many recognizable celebrities at Puck's "hatching" are the publishers of New York's leading newspapers. In the bottom-right corner of the cover, Thomas Nast takes a particularly grim view of the event.*

Joseph Keppler, *Puck*, April 17, 1878. *In 1878 New York City police arrested Madame Restell, a well known abortionist. The Puck cartoon suggests what will happen to the population count of one of the city's finer neighborhoods without her services, and in so doing comments on upperclass hypocrisy.*

FIFTH AVENUE FOUR YEARS AFTER MAD. RESTELL'S DEATH.

English; cartoon ideas had to be translated into German for his benefit.) How did these artists who didn't speak English conversationally—let alone fluently—hope to succeed with a magazine based on American politics and social mores? Keppler was so self-assured that *Puck's* first cover brashly thumbed its nose at the competition.

Initial sales were poor. Subscribers didn't know what to make of the mix of poetry, fiction, and comic humor. Advertisers, scant to begin with, by the seventh month had dwindled to a single column. For several years the magazine operated at a loss, sustained by profits from the German edition supported by New York's large German community. Shrewd business management by Schwarzmann, coupled with *Puck's* talented artists, helped the magazine survive and move from the barbershops of New York into its salons. By the early 1880s *Puck's* circulation had risen to 80,000, and in 1883 Keppler's financial interest in the magazine was placed at $600,000 by Keppler scholar and *Detroit News* cartoonist Draper Hill. As co-owner of the now successful magazines, Keppler reveled in artistic and political freedom in a way Nast never enjoyed.

Keppler exposed human pomposity and

self-righteousness wherever he found them. *Puck* delighted in zeroing in on satiric dissections of contemporary social issues. Keppler biographer Richard West lists many such topics: "The flawed jury system, preying plumbers, the death of a Fifth Avenue abortionist, life insurance fraud, female suffrage, the rising divorce rate....The result was an eclectic satire full of insight and humor, giving credence to the line from Shakespeare that had become the magazines motto: 'What fools these mortals be!'"

In the nineteenth century (as today), the materials from which the cartoonists mined their political similes and analogies were determined by their own interests and education and those of their audiences. A man crossed Niagara Falls on a tightrope, baseball became a fever, Coney Island became the popular summer gathering place, P. T. Barnum moved from museum owner to circus owner, a book about Uncle Tom became a bestseller—these were the current happenings that people talked about, and, hence, the events on which political cartoons were grafted.

The U.S. population in 1880 reached 50 million; by 1900 it would be 76 million, a gain of fifty percent in twenty years. Immigration peaked in 1882 when almost 800,000 foreigners arrived. These newcomers were an indispensable part of the thrust toward the twentieth century. Unskilled labor provided the work force; skilled labor brought refined European sensibilities and know-how and joined an educated middle class hungry for stimulation. The question of limiting immigration was often debated and Keppler, an immigrant himself, fueled the fires. Like Nast, he singled out the Irish Catholics for particularly caustic attacks, perpetuating the stereotypes

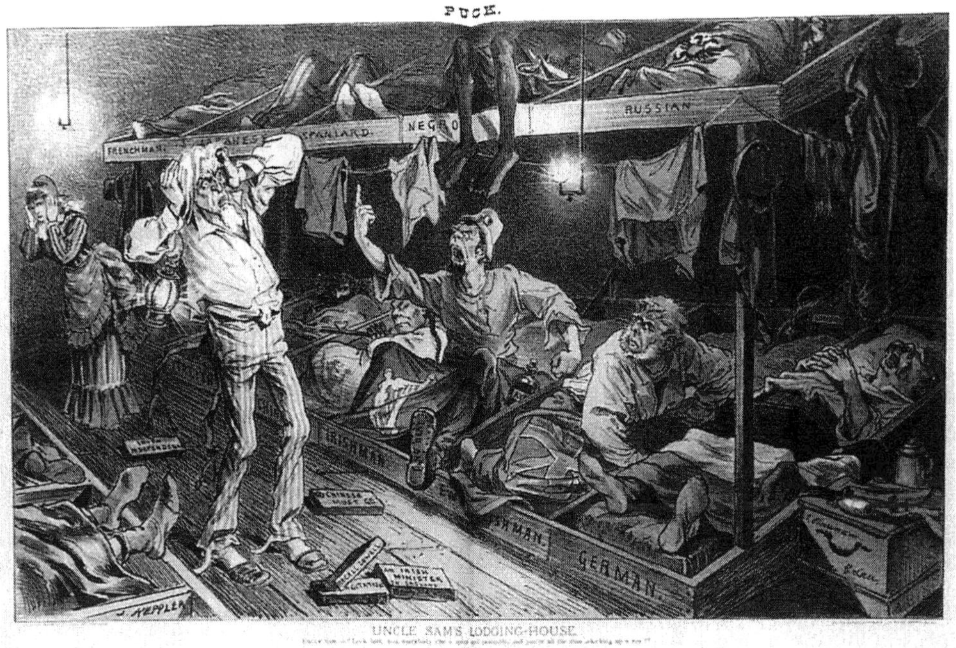

Joseph Keppler, *Puck*, June 7, 1882. *The accompanying editorial read: "The raw Irishman in America is a nuisance, his son a curse. They never assimilate; the second generation simply shows an intensification of all the bad qualities of the first.... They are a burden and a misery to this country. The time has come to clear the Irishman from the 'Uncle Sam's Lodging House,' where all the races and nationalities, except the Irish, get along with each other."*

James A. Wales (1852-86), ***Puck,*** **March 17, 1880. The 15-puzzle** ***was the rage of the day. Wales played off the game's popularity to show who was in the lead for the Republican presidential nomination. James Blaine and Samuel Tilden are so arranged on the board that whichever way the player moves, one seems bound to win. As it turned out, none of the contenders on Puck's puzzle board won. James Garfield would win both the nomination and the election.***

Nast had created, and damning their religion.

But it was Keppler's humorous perspective on American politics that sustained the magazine's popularity. Puck's first engagement in presidential politics began in a near-disastrous fashion. The magazine customarily had a ten-day gap between conception and publication of the massive color lithographs that were its trademark. In 1880, as the Republicans convened in Chicago, Puck artists began drawing "to meet every possible contingency." As an editorial stated, "We were ready for any nomination that the Convention could make—Grant, Blaine, Sherman, Washburne, Edmunds—it didn't matter; we had cartoons laid out for every one—even for the off-chance men—Private Dalzell and Hamilton Fish." On the thirty-sixth ballot the GOP finally made up its mind, and, unfortunately for Puck, it settled on a candidate whom the magazine had not considered—James A. Garfield. (The lesson learned from this experience was to run a puzzle cartoon when an election or nomination was in doubt.)

Four years later *Puck* showed the Republican presidential candidate, James G. Blaine, as a "Tattooed Man." On his body every charge ever made against the veteran politician

PHRYNE BEFORE THE CHICAGO TRIBUNAL

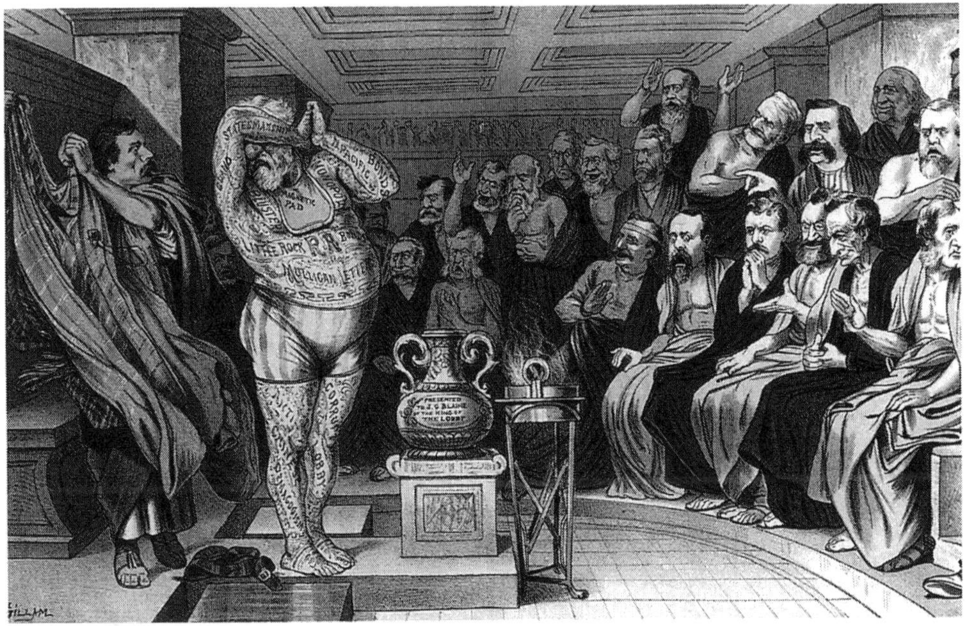

THE NAKED TRUTH

ABOVE: Bernard Gillam, *Puck*, June 4, 1884. ***The cartoon of James Blaine, the Republican presidential candidate, is a takeoff on a painting by the French artist Jean Léon Gérôme that had been a Paris sensation twelve years earlier. It is based on the story of the Greek orator Hyperides, who won a verdict for the courtesan Phryne by exposing her beauty to the court.***

LEFT: Paul Conrad, *Los Angeles Times*, February 17, 1987. ***Borrowing from Keppler's invention, Paul Conrad tattoos President Ronald Reagan with events stemming from his years in the White House.***

was engraved, including innuendos referring to Blaine's stock in a railroad holding company that had tried to influence pending legislation in Congress. It was a device Keppler had used when he worked for *Frank Leslie's Illustrated.* This time Bernard Gillam, a talented British artist Keppler had lured away from *Leslie's Illustrated,* did the tattooing. The cartoon proved an instant sensation. Blaine was furious and wanted to sue *Puck* for libel, and only strong pressure from his friends dissuaded him from going to court. Perhaps the grandest irony of the cartoon was that Gillam was a staunch Republican and actually voted for Blaine.

Puck's rival, *Judge* was founded in 1881 by James Wales who left *Puck* after a quarrel with Keppler. Wales attempted to make his publication nonpartisan, but was never able to put

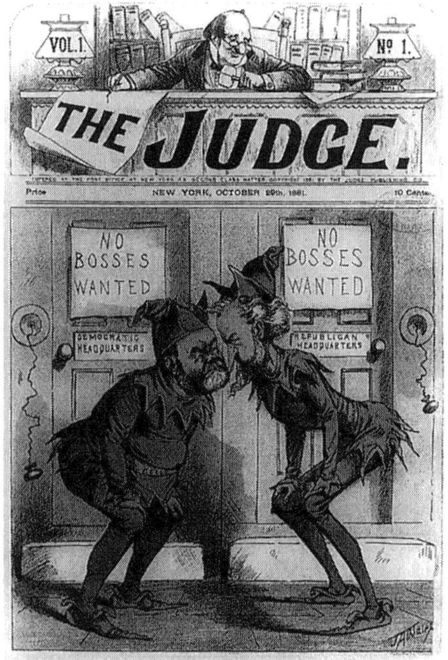

THE TWO POLITICAL DROMIOS.
What are we going to do about it?

"BENJAMIN—WHERE AM I AT?"

LEFT: James A. Wales, *Judge*, October 29, 1881. RIGHT: Bernard Gillam, *Judge*, November 19, 1892. *Convinced that Benjamin Harrison would win reelection in 1892, Gillam prepared a double-page cartoon of Grover Cleveland being run over by the GOP elephant, which was on the press when the news of the Democrats' smashing victory reached the Judge office. Gillam quickly doctored the cut, changing Cleveland's face to Harrison's, adding an "Overwhelming Defeat" eye patch to the elephant, and generally trying to make his drawing reflect the altered situation. Perhaps to show the quick turnaround, Gillam pictured himself as a monkey turning a somersault in the lower-left corner.*

Judge on firm financial footing. He sold the magazine to William J. Arkell in 1885 and returned to Keppler's stable. The new owner promptly lured Bernard Gillam away from *Puck* by making him a full partner. They turned *Judge* into a Republican journal to counter Democratic *Puck.*

Two years after the founding *of Judge,* the last of the great triumvirate of late-nineteenth-century humor magazines made its appearance. *Life* entered the field in 1883 with not only the bubbling enthusiasm of the very young but also a sophistication that belied its founders' years. *Life* (an earlier, distinct magazine from the current publication) was the product of *Harvard Lampoon* graduates, and its first issues bore a striking resemblance to the college humor magazine. Its guiding spirit was John Ames Mitchell, known to his artists as "The General." The magazine would focus mainly on social issues. Perhaps more than any other magazine, *Life* chronicled the volatile question of women's suffrage, alternately supporting and rejecting the idea.

It is hard to overestimate the political influence of *Puck* and its rival, *Judge,* during the last two decades of the nineteenth century. One observer thought it greater than all the

THE NEW NAVY

THE COMING MAN:
"TELL HER I'LL BE RIGHT DOWN."

ABOVE: William H. Walker, *Life*, April 16, 1896. *William Walker, one of* Life's *most respected cartoonists, produced a series of tableaux in which strident, fat, unattractive women dressed in puffy bloomers usurp men's roles. Men's horror of sexually aggressive women was only topped by the fear of getting stuck at home with the kids.*

LEFT: *Life*, March 25, 1896. Life's *artists delighted in using role-reversal gags: women became aggressors, and men were reduced to wimps.*

Joseph Keppler, *Puck*, January 23, 1889.

daily newspapers combined: "Their weekly cartoons were awaited eagerly, were passed from hand to hand, and were the subject of animated comment in all political circles." When Keppler suggested the establishment of an independent party in 1882, his challenge was taken seriously. Two years later, he abandoned the idea and supported Grover Cleveland. Many readers felt Keppler had been co-opted by the political deals he was known to abhor.

The last two decades of the nineteenth century were a time of competitive and fierce economic expansion. Trusts grew up in every industry. Wielding enormous economic power, these giants soon had Congress working for their benefit. Between 1881 and 1905 there were 37,000 labor strikes including bloody confrontations in the railroad and steel industries. Cartoonists like Keppler, who had originally supported the workingman, turned against labor as the violence continued. Few cartoonists remarked on the incidents, the conditions that created the violence, or the plight of the underclass. Instead, they aimed their attacks on the all-pervasive power of the trusts, monopolies, and big business.

In 1893 the Columbian Exposition opened in Chicago to celebrate the 400th anniversary of Columbus's discovery of America. The fair celebrated outstanding achievements in technology, and Joseph Keppler was invited to participate because of the contributions he had made by introducing color lithography to publishing. Keppler commissioned architect Stanford White to design a glorious pavilion at the fair from which a weekly special edition was published. Thousands of visitors packed the pavilion to see *Puck's* huge presses turn and to meet its editor.

Strolling along the midway under the shadow of the first Ferris wheel were other cartoonists hired to illustrate the spectacular events for daily newspapers—Thomas Nast and Arthur Young for the *Chicago Inter-Ocean* and John McCutcheon of the *Chicago Record.* But the tourists seemed interested in recording the events for themselves using a simple, easy-to-use Kodak camera. The Exposition would be the last major spectacle to be illustrated by hand.

Fleeing the summer's relentless heat, Keppler returned to New York exhausted and never regained his strength. He died the following winter at age fifty-six. *Puck* would continue to publish until 1918 with Joseph Keppler Jr. as one of its principal artists, but its day at the forefront of American publishing and politics was over.

Thomas Nast eked out a living by freelancing for another decade, but his popularity had long since diminished. His drawings seemed out of step with the times and were often rejected. His investments and business enterprises soured. After making a career out of criticizing government, Nast accepted a modest position as U.S. consul to Guayaquil, Ecuador (in order "to learn how to pronounce its name," he said). He would die there in December 1902 of yellow fever, only seven months after arriving at the post. His body was not returned to the United States for burial until 1906.

Nast left no disciples or school of cartooning; still, in a sense, every cartoonist was his student, freely adopting the symbols he invented and, more importantly, experiencing greater acceptance because there had been a Thomas Nast. Joseph Keppler is as unknown to cartoonists as he is to the general public, yet his contributions to the profession are equally important. Besides introducing brilliant, living color to American publishing, he brought to his drawings a blithe attitude that embraced and critiqued humankind in the same breath. It is this elusive combination that continues to endear cartoons to each new generation.

Volcanoes Cannot Stop Thomas Nast

Thomas Nast, pencil sketch, 1902.
En route to his assignment in Ecuador, Nast sketched this drawing for a friend.

THE CARTOON COMES OF AGE: 1896 - 1918

AS THE UNITED STATES CAREENED into the twentieth century, the spirit of innovation driving the nation was mirrored in the business of cartooning. There were more newspapers, faster presses, greater competition, and, in many cities, cartoons reigned on the front page. Political cartoons and comic strips sold newspapers, and the cartoonists who drew them—now numbering nearly 2,000—became well-known celebrities, frequently called upon to lead parades, propose toasts, and cut ribbons. The techniques they developed and the styles that evolved to meet daily deadlines would dominate the medium for the next seventy-five years.

Three years before Keppler founded *Puck* in 1876, Frederick Hudson had stated in his *History of Journalism* that the American public did not support comic weeklies because "no one can wait a week to laugh; it must come in daily with our coffee." Yet until the 1880s one form of humor, the cartoon, was notable for its absence in the daily newspaper. True, there had been occasional newspaper cartoons ever since Benjamin Franklin's "Join, or Die," but cartoons were expensive and painfully slow to produce. Newspaper type, moreover, was set in narrow columns and the presses made it inconvenient to print anything larger than one column in width—a space too confining for an effective cartoon.

Newsboys, Lewis Hine (1874-1940), February 12, 1908.

In 1867 James Gordon Bennett Jr. founded the *New York Evening Telegram.* Printed on pink paper and featuring gory murders and sexual escapades, Bennett's product, wrote biographer Richard O'Conner, "obviously was designed to appeal to readers who tended to move their lips when they read it." The *Telegram* also ran a big front-page cartoon every Friday, making the newspaper the first daily in the country to use cartoons on a regular basis.

The great breakthrough for the newspaper cartoon came five days before the presidential election of 1884 when Joseph Pulitzer's *New York World* printed "The Royal Feast of Belshazzar," a front-page cartoon satirizing a dinner held the night before to honor the Republican candidate, James G. Blaine. Walt McDougall played off a biblical story, and the drawing showed the candidate hobnobbing with his high-powered cronies while a family's pleas for some food from the well-stocked table go ignored. The cartoon created a sensation. The Democrats reproduced it on thousands of

READ THE SIXTH PAGE.
CIRCULATION OVER 100,000 EVERY DAY.
ADVERTISE YOUR WANTS.
Cheapest Rates in the City.

The World.

VOL. XXV., NO. 8,472. NEW YORK, THURSDAY, OCTOBER 30, 1884.—WITH SUPPLEMENT. PRICE TWO CENTS.

THE ROYAL FEAST OF BELSHAZZAR BLAINE AND THE MONEY KINGS.

MAMMON'S HOMAGE.

Blaine Hobnobbing With the Mighty Money Kings.

The Banquet in His Honor at Delmonico's Last Night.

Millionaires and Monopolists Seal Their Allegiance.

Walt McDougall, *New York World*, October 30, 1884. ***Although crude and artless in its rendering, this cartoon overshadowed Puck's "Tattooed Man" series that ran concurrently. Walt McDougall was the lead cartoonist, but many of the faces were drawn by Valerian Gribayedoff, a Russian-born soldier of fortune and specialist in portraiture.***

billboards in the Empire State. Blaine would have been elected if he had carried New York, but he lost the state by a mere 1,100 votes. Many said the cartoon was responsible for putting Grover Cleveland in the White House.

Hungarian-born Joseph Pulitzer had founded the *St. Louis Post-Dispatch* in 1878 and entered the more competitive New York newspaper market in 1883, buying the *New York World.* Determined to turn his new paper into a national force by making it the spokesman for the workingman, he dressed the *World* in lively, eye-catching graphics: news illustrations, cartoons, and comics. Pulitzer's success taunted the ambitious young publisher of the *San Francisco Examiner,* William Randolph Hearst, who while a student at Harvard had followed Pulitzer's endeavors. In 1895 Hearst bought the moribund *New York Journal* for $180,000. In the great circulation war that followed, the cost of newspapers plummeted to one cent a copy. Where once subscribers shouldered the cost of publications, advertisers now became the chief source of revenue.

Hearst used his family's vast resources to hire away some of Pulitzer's best talent, including Richard Outcault, creator of "Hogan's Alley," which had become the *World's* biggest draw on Sundays. The strip featured the "Yellow Dugan Kid," a toothless, hairless, street urchin in a

RIGHT: Frederick Opper (1857-1937), reprinted in *New York Times*, October 1, 1967. *Although Pulitzer would lose to Hearst in the battle for primacy of the cartoon pages, his journalism settled into responsible reporting. The prestigious Pulitzer Prizes are presented in his name.*

FAR RIGHT: W. A. Rogers (1854-1931), *Harper's Weekly*, October 27, 1906. *Hearst's political ambitions are made clear in this cartoon, as he steps over the Albany state capitol heading for the White House.*

ATLAS JOE; OR, THE FEARFUL RESPONSIBILITIES OF A SELF-APPOINTED MANAGER OF THE UNIVERSE.

ONLY A STEPPING-STONE

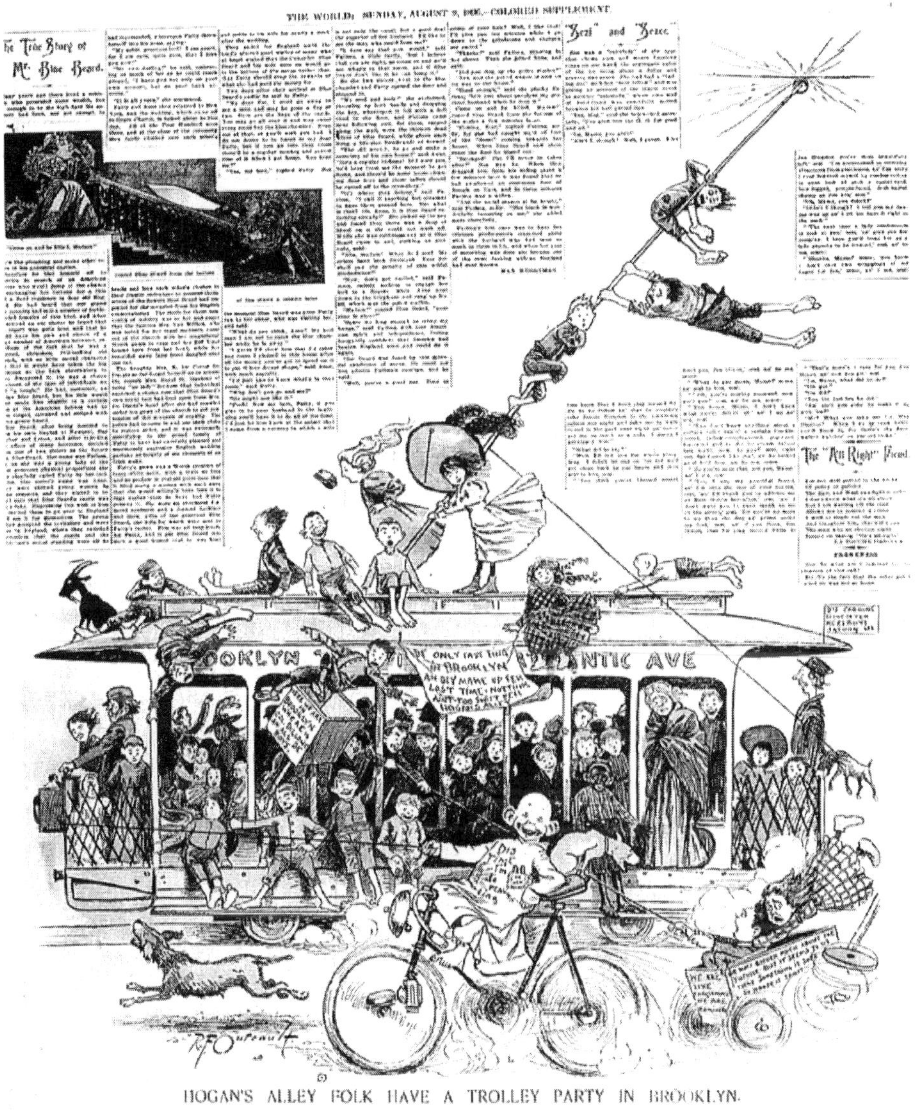

HOGAN'S ALLEY FOLK HAVE A TROLLEY PARTY IN BROOKLYN.

ABOVE: Library of Congress registration of Outcault's "Yellow Dugan Kid," September 2, 1896. ***Richard Outcault applied to the Library of Congress in 1896 for a copyright for the Yellow Kid. He derived a healthy income licensing his creation for all types of advertisements.***

LEFT: Richard Outcault (1863-1928), ***New York World,*** **August 11, 1896.**

RIGHT: Self-caricature, Richard Outcault, ***Everybody's Magazine,*** **circa 1896.**

THE BIG TYPE WAR OF THE YELLOW KIDS

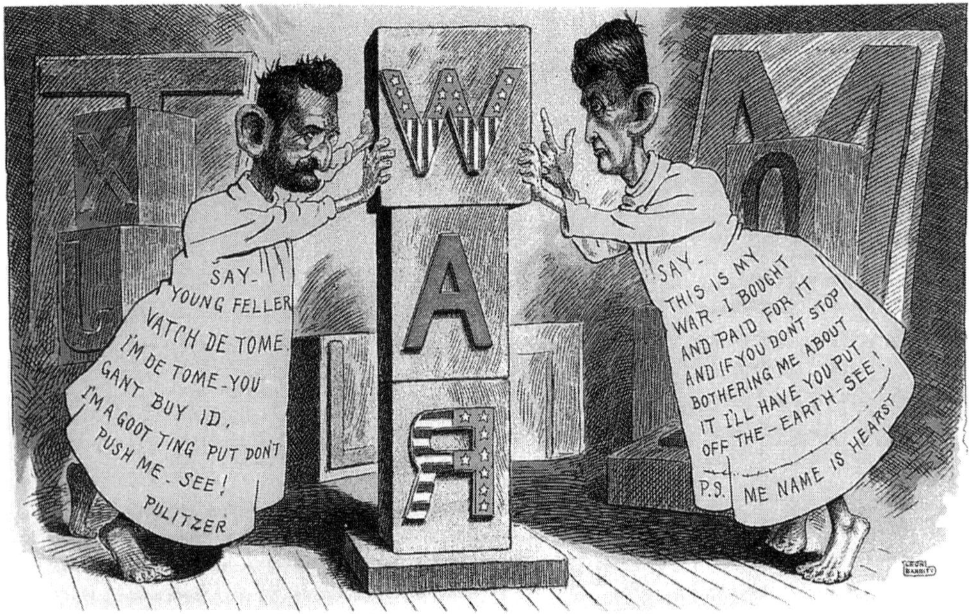

Leon Barritt (1852-1938), *Vim*, June 29, 1898. *As Pulitzer and Hearst lobbied for war, the size of the type used grew larger, until an entire front page was often consumed by only two or three words. Cartoonist Leon Barritt cleverly dressed the dueling publishers in the distinctive garb of the Yellow Kid, from which the term yellow journalism was derived.*

yellow nightgown who each week took readers on fanciful escapades in and around the backyards of New York. The kid was Irish and was often joined in the panel by children of every other possible heritage, who seemed to carry little of their parents' prejudice.

Outcault's cartoon was the first to clearly increase newspaper sales for its host paper. When Pulitzer lost Outcault, he continued "Hogan's Alley" with artist George Luks. Litigation between Pulitzer and Hearst ensued. A court later decreed that Pulitzer had the right to continue the series under its original title and Outcault could draw his copyrighted kid for whomever he wished.

An insurrection in Cuba that had been simmering for several years came to a head in 1898 with the sinking of the American battleship *Maine* in Havana's harbor, precipitating the Spanish-American War. The conflict provided Hearst and Pulitzer with the excuse for a rip-roaring circulation-building crusade. Hearst's artists drew fake atrocity pictures of Spaniards stripping American women on the high seas, while Pulitzer's correspondents in Cuba cabled reports of "Blood on the roadsides, blood in the fields, blood on the doorsteps, blood, blood, blood." Sales of Hearst's *Journal* shot up to more than one million copies a day and Pulitzer's *World* followed closely with an 860,000 daily average. (In contrast, at its peak circulation in 1884, *Puck* had sold 125,000 magazines weekly.)

In 1899 Hearst lured Frederick Burr Opper to the *Journal.* Opper had spent eighteen years with *Puck,* and would remain with the Hearst organization for thirty-two years. Opper's early work was highly imitative of Keppler, but *Puck's* huge lithographic canvases were ill suited to his comic talents. It was only when he turned to smaller pen-and-ink drawings that his own style emerged—a style that one reviewer described as "a mixture of barbed wire and chicken scratches." Opper did two popular series that assured his fame: "Willie and His Poppa" and "Nursery Rhymes for Infant Industries." The continuing exploits of Willie (McKinley) and Teddy (Roosevelt) were eagerly awaited in the Roosevelt household, the Rough Rider told cartoonist W A. Rogers, and "His children got no end of amusement out of them, too." Opper's cartoons on trusts featured "Mr. Common People." The series ended with this poem:

With these alphabet pictures
the artist took pains,
But he's got to stop now,
and with grief nearly busts
'Cause our language but
twenty-six letters contains,
Though our country contains
twenty-six hundred trusts.

For many cartoonists the transition from magazines to newspapers was difficult, often impossible. The leisurely routine of the weekly journals was replaced by a grinding, daily demand. Many artists quickly found they could not stand the pace or the increased drain on their creative juices. Moreover, the different media required different techniques. In terms of both the artist's time and the lack of sophis-

OPPER AS A MAN OF THE STONE AGE

LEFT: Frederick Opper, *New York American and Journal*, September 27, 1902.

ABOVE: Upjohn, *Everybody's Magazine*, June 1905.

tication of newspaper reproduction, it was impossible to use the intricate group portraits that had been the staple of *Puck* and *Judge* or the elaborate backdrops in which the caricatures were placed. Opper was one of the few men to make the transition comfortably. Most of the newspapers would turn to a new generation of cartoonists.

The first of the major figures to come of age in newspaper cartooning was Homer Davenport. He and Opper became Hearst's one-two punch. But, unlike the gentle Opper,

Davenport's pictures "invite battle and tears," wrote editor Horace Traubel. Davenport was a bruiser whose best blow was a roundhouse to the midsection. Born in Silverton, Oregon, Davenport was to play the role of "country boy" even after he became New York's highest-paid cartoonist. "The funniest things happen to me," he said. "I am always being taken for my coachman, or a groom in my stable, or some sort of a servant."

MARK HANNA AS HE IS AND AS DAVENPORT MADE HIM.

A MAN OF MARK!

Hearst had first employed Davenport on the *San Francisco Examiner* and brought him East in time for the 1896 presidential campaign. Hearst's *New York Journal* was the only major newspaper in the country to support Democrat William Jennings Bryan against Republican William McKinley. McKinley's campaign manager was Cleveland industrialist Mark Hanna, who was to become as well known as the candidate he represented.

Hanna and Hearst were both masters of the art of manipulation. As Bryan, a heretofore political unknown, embarked on a crowd-pleasing, cross-country tour, Hanna had his

ABOVE LEFT: Homer Davenport, *New York Journal*, November 8, 1896. *Hanna and Davenport finally met after the 1896 election. The politician supposedly said, "I admire your execution but damn your conception." Davenport made these sketches at that meeting.*

ABOVE RIGHT: Homer Davenport, *New York Journal*, August 4, 1896.

LEFT: Self-caricature, Homer Davenport, *Cartoon* magazine, circa 1900.

OPPOSITE: Homer Davenport, *New York Journal*, November 4, 1900.

TO CYCLERS!!

READ TO-MORROW'S JOURNAL FOR SOMETHING THAT WILL INTEREST YOU.

NEW YORK JOURNAL

WHEELWOMEN!!

YOU MUST NOT FAIL TO READ THE JOURNAL TO-MORROW. DON'T MISS IT!

PRICE ONE CENT.

BRYAN GREETED IN M'KINLEY'S STATE.

Democratic Candidate Given an Enthusiastic Welcome.

A Hundred Thousand Cheering Voters Turn Out in Cleveland.

WILD SPOTTED BEAST ATE UP STRAY DOGS.

Had Escaped from a Circus and Was Thought to Be a Bengal Tiger.

VERMONT NAMES A GOVERNOR TO-DAY.

Senator Merrill Claims the State for Republicans by 35,000.

WALL STREET WISHES A NEW GUARDIAN OF THE TREASURY.

candidate stay home and conduct his campaign from his front porch in Canton, Ohio, arranging for delegations to come to him. McKinley was the last of a generation of Civil War officers to run for president and had an unblemished record in politics. Knowing that the candidate was virtually unassailable, Hearst attacked Hanna instead, using the power of the cartoon as his main weapon. Davenport turned the Republican campaign manager into an image of greed and manipulation that would haunt him for the rest of his life.

Although the clever use of caricature was the artist's, the message was that of the publisher Hearst who nurtured his own political ambitions and would have liked to become the Democratic nominee for president. Davenport distorted Hanna's features in much the same way Nast had transformed Tweed's. The artist wrote in 1899 in an article entitled "The Gentle Art of Making the Wicked Squirm": "Hanna's eyes are inclined to be small and keen ... and without detracting any from his character of face the artist can draw them much smaller.... His nose is short and very stout at the base, and with a rise at the point. This also can be nicely exaggerated.... His ears are big and as shapely as well developed pie plant leaves....In general make-up [Hanna], while a rather competent-looking businessman, has a coarse appearance, and to make him a little coarser helps the cartoon, which is, in brief, merely an exaggeration of certain truths." Davenport eventually left the *Journal* and was employed by the Republican Party. Here was one cartoonist who could be bought.

The popularity of cartooning in the daily newspapers was not limited to New York City. At the turn of the century Albert Shaw, editor of Review of Reviews, wrote: "There is now not a town of any size in the country that has not a paper utilizing the services of a cartoonist." Although the best of these artists were sometimes lured to the New York dailies, a number of other regions developed and retained their own voices. In the years to come the syndica-

LEFT: Nelson Harding (1879-1947), ***Brooklyn Eagle*****, January 18, 1908. CENTER: Robert Minor (1884-1952),** ***St. Louis Post-Dispatch*****, reprinted in** ***Cartoons*** **magazine, July 1912. RIGHT: Rollin Kirby (1875-1952),** ***New York World*****, May 19, 1925.** ***For more than thirty years, William Jennings Bryan captured the imagination of writers and artists. His quest for the presidency became a recurring theme in cartoons that chronicled Bryan's evolution from the handsome thirty-six-year-old "Boy Orator of the Platte" who swept the 1896 Democratic convention to the bloated, balding old man who opposed the teaching of Darwinian theory at the famous Scopes trial of 1925.***

tion of cartoonists' work, an enterprise started by Hearst's editor, Arthur Brisbane, would undermine the role of regional cartoonists. But the first two decades of the twentieth century saw local cartoonists mount sustained attacks against hometown corruption, mismanagement, and fraud with devastating accuracy. William A. Ireland, a first-ranked cartoonist on the *Columbus (Ohio) Dispatch* for many years, constantly refused offers from papers in greater metropolitan areas. He explained, "My object isn't to break into New York; it is to break back to Chillicothe."

In Chicago, a town known for its outstanding pool of cartoon talent, *Chicago Tribune* cartoonist John T. McCutcheon reigned as "the first man of Chicago." McCutcheon approached his subjects with joy, seeking to reinforce the good he saw around him. His characters were reminiscent of his own boyhood in Indiana. They were good people—perhaps a little too good—and together they strolled into the twentieth century on a rainbow of optimism, trading the rural lifestyle for urbanity and the problems that accompanied it. He wrote: "I always enjoyed drawing a type of cartoon which might be considered a sort of pictorial breakfast food. It had the cardinal asset of making the beginning of a day sunnier. It is safe to say that the prairies were not set afire by these cartoons, yet they had the merit of offending no one." Many of McCutcheon's cartoons today read like a time capsule of the era.

McCutcheon joined the *Chicago Tribune* in 1903, after spending a decade at the *Chicago Daily Record.* He remained at the paper for more than forty-three years. Although McCutcheon also drew many hard-hitting cartoons, he is remembered for his cartoon homilies that offered comforting antidotes to the news that surrounded them. Author George Ade wrote of his friend: "McCutcheon realizes the fact that political events do not fill the entire horizon of the American people. We admire the gentle humor that diffuses his work, but I dare say, more than all, we admire him for his blessed wisdom in getting away from hackneyed political subjects and giving us a few pictures of everyday life."

There was one phenomenon that

Self-caricature, John T. McCutcheon (1870-1949), *Drawn from Memory*, 1950. *John McCutcheon's studio in the top of the tower of the Chicago Tribune Building was filled with mementos from his travels around the world. McCutcheon would often take leave from his drawing board and venture to exotic lands, sometimes reporting on breaking news events for the paper. He once joined Teddy Roosevelt on safari in Africa.*

ABOVE: John McCutcheon, *Chicago Tribune*, October 9-10, 1903.

RIGHT: Leon Barritt, *Vim*, 1898.

McCutcheon and Barritt show contrasting points of view. While McCutcheon depicts families enjoying a vast array of goods, Barritt shows a bat standing upon the skulls of smaller merchants put out of business by the rise of department stores.

McCutcheon and the other turn-of-the-century artists could always count on to make their lives easier: Theodore Roosevelt. Catapulted to national attention leading the First Volunteer Cavalry— the Rough Riders—in Cuba in 1898, Roosevelt began a spectacular climb in Republican politics. He rose from New York governor to Vice President and assumed the presidency when McKinley was fatally shot in 1901. The Rough Rider president expanded the powers of the presidency and the federal government. He was instrumental in containing the trusts and in negotiating between big business and labor.

Roosevelt was himself a frustrated cartoonist (as seen from the sketches with which he peppered his delightful letters to his children), and he rarely took offense at even the most outrageous crimes that the cartooning fraternity perpetrated against his features. In fact, sportsman Roosevelt was known to have been publicly irritated by just one cartoon (in the *Wichita Eagle),* and then only because it showed him mounting a war horse with the wrong foot in the stirrup.

THE PRESIDENTIAL HOLIDAY

HE ARRIVES IN "SAN ANTONE" TO ATTEND A REUNION OF THE ROUGH RIDERS

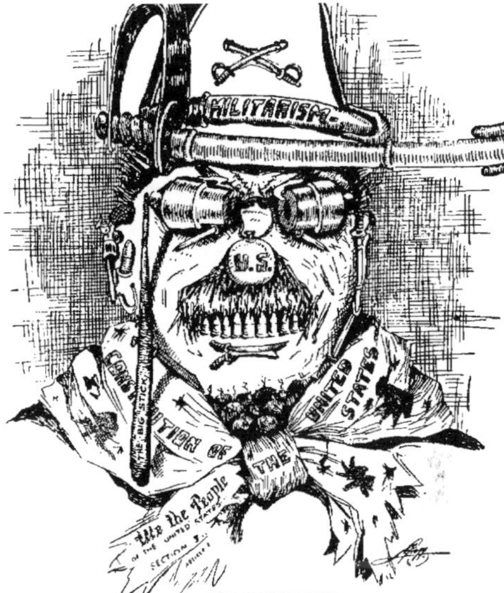

FOR PRESIDENT

WHERE TEDDY'S ANNOUNCEMENT CAUSED JOY

ABOVE: L.C. Gregg, *Atlanta Constitution*, 1904.

FAR LEFT: John McCutcheon, *Chicago Tribune*, April 6, 1905.

LEFT: A.W. Brewerton (1881-1960), *Atlanta Journal*, February 27, 1912.

ABOVE: Caricature of Robert Minor, Art Young, *Good Morning*, May 1921.

RIGHT: Robert Minor, *St. Louis Post-Dispatch*, reprinted in *Cartoon* magazine, circa 1912.

WHY WOMEN WANT TO VOTE

Besides having a talent for self-dramatization, Roosevelt was a master wordsmith whose ability to invent phrases like "my hat's in the ring," "rough riders," "speak softly and carry a big stick," "muckrakers," and "I feel like a bull moose," would provide the cartoonists with a steady diet of new symbols.

In stark contrast to John McCutcheon, in both style and content, was the work of Robert Minor, cartoonist for Pulitzer's *St. Louis Post-Dispatch* and *New York World* and later for *The Masses.* A quiet Texan from an educated but poor family, Minor had worked on the rails (becoming a union member in good standing) long before he discovered that he could make a living from his art. When he joined the *Post-Dispatch* in 1905, his first art assignment was to make sketches of each morning's fresh corpses at the city morgue, which then accompanied the grizzly stories of the victims' deaths. His salary was $18 a week. By the time he left in 1912 he had become the country's highest-paid cartoonist. Where other cartoonists used elaborate crosshatching, Minor made a radical departure, discarding the delicate lines of pen and ink in favor of a broad, crude, grease crayon. When the *Post-Dispatch's* pressmen first saw Minor's new crayon style they declared it unprintable. Refusing to be dissuaded, the artist went down to the presses and worked with them until a successful method for transferring his drawings to print was achieved. Minor's bold, emotive cartoons were soon widely imitated.

The young Texan's passionate socialist convictions further distinguished his work. Minor's cartoons focused on the working-class struggle. By 1912 Eugene Debs's Socialist Party had more than 118,000 members who had elected more than 1,000 of their ranks to public office. Although certainly not in the mainstream of American politics, the socialist philosophy was accepted if not embraced. That Minor's sympathy for their ideals could be accommodated and applauded by the readers and the management of the *Post-Dispatch* shows the degree of accommodation most of America had at that time to the movement.

In 1911 Ralph Pulitzer, son of Joseph Pulitzer, invited the twenty-seven-year-old artist to move from his St. Louis paper and join his *New York World* staff, but Minor had other ideas: he wanted to study art in Europe. According to Minor biographer Joseph North, the two men reached an agreement, and the cartoonist went to France on a year's hiatus with a generous advance from his employer. What he learned in that year would change the course of his life: his drawings and ideals grew stronger from studying the works of Daumier and Doré, but more importantly, his political beliefs were now driven by a commitment to the doctrine of anarchy then popular in Europe.

PITTSBURGH, 1916

Robert Minor, *The Masses*, 1916.

Minor returned home just as war was breaking out on the European Continent in 1914 and settled into his new job at the *New York World.* The paper had supported President Wilson, who had promised to keep America out of the war, and adopted an editorial position against the conflict. Minor was given free rein, and over the next two years he produced many powerful cartoons that had as their theme the belief that the escalating war in Europe was being waged by bankers and industrialists for their own profit. But as death and devastation spread over Europe, the *World,* like most major newspapers of the day, took up the call for American intervention. Minor refused to draw prowar cartoons and was eventually fired.

Most American cartoonists, however, stood behind the United States' entry into the war in April 1917. In 1918 a Bureau of Cartoons was set up under the auspices of the government to mobilize the cartoonists for the war effort. The bureau

COMMITTEE ON PUBLIC INFORMATION

GEORGE CREEL, Chairman
THE SECRETARY OF STATE
THE SECRETARY OF WAR
THE SECRETARY OF THE NAVY

Bureau of Cartoons — Bulletin No. 20

BULLETIN FOR CARTOONISTS

OCTOBER 26, 1918

"THAT'S MY FIGHT, TOO!"

LEFT: James Montgomery Flagg, *Bulletin for Cartoonists*, October 26, 1918.

RIGHT: Rollin Kirby, *New York World*, 1917.

published a weekly *Bulletin for Cartoonists* that listed fitting subjects and often came close to providing the pictorial ideas themselves. After Congress passed the draft-registration bill, the August 31, 1918, *Bulletin* declared: "You, the cartoonists of the country, have here an opportunity to be of immeasurable aid to the Government....Through your cartoons you can inspire in every man a keen sense of his obligation to the cause of democracy and stimulate public opinion on this vital issue as few other forces in this country can."

Patriotism replaced originality, and cartoonists became little more than government cheerleaders, stimulating recruitment, popularizing the draft, and selling war bonds.

Perhaps the most significant cartoonist in the American press during the war was not an American at all but a Dutchman, Louis Raemaekers, whose work appeared originally in the *Amsterdam Telegraaf.* Before the war was over, the German government had put a price on his head, the Dutch government had prosecuted him for endangering its neutrality (he was acquitted), and there was even a report that the Germans had attempted to torpedo the ship on which he left Holland for exile in England. Raemaekers's pictures often combined a haunting beauty with a biting satire. In the United States his cartoons were widely reproduced in the Hearst papers.

One group of American cartoonists took a consistently pacifist position even after the United States had entered the war. Their opinions appeared in journals of minuscule circulation, and their influence on the public at large was virtually nil. As artists, however, they were doing work that was generally well above the caliber seen in the popular press. These were the radicals. Some, like Robert Minor, called themselves anarchists. Most were socialists.

Their primary showcase was *The Masses* (1911-17), a handsome Greenwich Village magazine whose circulation averaged 12,000. Its issues were packed with large illustrations commenting on a wide range of social issues. Under the editorship of Max Eastman the magazine became one of the liveliest publications of the era.

The first art editor of *The Masses* was painter John Sloan who recruited other talented artists, including George Bellows and

ON THE WHITE HORSE

Louis Raemaekers (1869-1956), 1917.

"O WICKED FLESH"

ABOVE: **Robert Minor, *The Masses*, August 1916.** ***One reader admonished the goals of The Masses in poetry: "They drew fat women for the Masses, Denuded, fat, ungainly lasses—How does that help the working classes?"***

FAR RIGHT: John Sloan (1871-1951), *The Masses*, July 1913. ***Sloan's working women stand in stark contrast to the stylish drawings of Charles Dana Gibson (1867-1944) popular at the turn of the century*** **(RIGHT).**

RETURN FROM TOIL

John Sloan, *The Masses*, June 1913.

Boardman Robinson (1876-1952), *The Masses*, October 1916.

Stuart Davis. In weekly meetings the contributors would decide whose work would be included in the monthly magazine. For many of *The Masses'* artists it was an opportunity to publish their best work, work that had been turned down by mainstream publications because of its political content. Stories with illustrations about working women, striking miners, and the children of the ghettos abounded. Censorship of any kind was given a sharp rebuke. Yet as progressive as the group's views were, they failed to see that their drawings of African Americans were, at best, benevolent but demeaning stereotypes.

One artist in the group of *Masses* contributors stands out. If Max Eastman was the brains behind *The Masses,* then Art Young became its soul. Young's fervent commitment to the ideals of socialism was equaled by his joyous humor and distinctive style. Painter Peggy Bacon described Young as "honest, mild, and merry but armed to the teeth with talent and sardonic knowledge. A kindhearted soldier with a machine gun." *The Masses* would be a brief, happy interlude for Young in a career that was troubled by a failure to find a permanent base.

Young became *The Masses'* art editor in 1916, when a rift developed with Sloan over the captioning of cartoons. Sloan and his sup-

Having Their Fling

Art Young, *The Masses*, September 1917.

porters wanted their work to run without captions, art for art's sake. Young and other contributors felt that art should be used as a weapon; that every picture appearing in the magazine should state its political position clearly. Young said, "They want to run pictures of ash cans and girls hitching up their skirts in Horatio Street—regardless of ideas—and without titles [captions]....For my part, I do not care to be connected with a publication that does not try to point the way out of a sordid materialistic world." Sloan and the others resigned. Young was joined by Robert Minor and Boardman Robinson. Together, they would produce powerful anti-war statements as World War I approached.

The belligerent antiwar posture of *The Masses* led to its suppression by the U.S. government in 1917. Art Young, Max Eastman, and three others were brought to trial under the Espionage Act, which made it a crime to say or write anything critical of the war effort. Young's cartoons were specifically cited. Said Eastman, "They give you ninety days for quoting the Declaration of Independence, six months for quoting the Bible, and pretty soon somebody is going to get a life sentence for quoting Woodrow Wilson in the wrong context." The two trials of *The Masses* staff ended in hung juries, but the magazine did not survive. The zeal that had nourished it was gone.

But for a brief time, wrote literary critic Irving Howe, "*The Masses* became the rallying point for almost everything that was then alive and irreverent in American culture." *The Masses* was superseded by a series of socialist magazines. As the radical left became more communist and doctrinaire, the quality of its humor degenerated into heavy-handed propaganda. Robert Minor would leave cartooning to become a candidate and spokesperson for the Communist Party.

Daily cartooning had become part of American life. The cartoonists who were part of this transition demonstrated just how powerful good cartoons could be. They had helped elect presidents and send soldiers to war, and they had elevated the level of debate on many social issues. Whether the artists were mainstream or socialist, their cartoons became striking, often humorous, statements of their beliefs. By the end of World War I, however, cartoons were being moved off of the front pages of newspapers where they had reigned for decades. They were placed on the editorial page and were reduced in size. An era was over.

FREEDOM OF THE PRESS

ABOVE: Self-caricature, Art Young, *The Masses*, December 1915.

RIGHT: Art Young, *The Masses*, December 1912. *Young started as a cartoonist for the conservative Chicago Inter-Ocean in 1884. He moved to New York City four years later and with his fiery, funny cartoon style became a respected freelance contributor to publications like* Life, Puck, *and* Hearst's New York Journal. *Young joined the Socialist Party in 1910 and from then on his beliefs and his career were in conflict. He wanted to draw cartoons that reflected his point of view, but mainstream publications showed little interest in running work that skewered capitalism. Young vehemently criticized the mainstream press for compromising its news reporting to please advertisers, as the cartoon "Freedom of the Press" suggests. These tenaciously held views made jobs hard to come by in his later years. Other cartoonists who admired Young and his work often chipped in to pay his outstanding bills. Young retired to a farm in Connecticut where he wrote two autobiographies notable for their mirth and optimism despite a lifetime of seeing his best work go unpublished. He died there in 1943.*

THE ART OF UNCERTAINTY: 1918 - 1947

THE END OF WORLD WAR I sent America on a roller-coaster ride that would last nearly thirty years, through boom and bust, war and cold war. The pace of change was dramatic and many cartoonists, caught up in its capricious whirlwind, opted for gags to cover their own uncertainty over where the ride was taking them. Bathtub gin and flappers, Al Capone and Lucky Lindy, Hollywood's and radio's Amos and Andy were easier to visualize than a failed peace plan, a bullish stock market, or growing unemployment. Yet a few distinct voices pushed forward the tradition of visual political commentary. President Woodrow Wilson's peace plan, with its call for a League of Nations, was the first test of the cartoonists' mettle in postwar America.

THE CASH REGISTER CHORUS

LEFT: John Held Jr. (1889-1958), *Sheik with Sheba*, 1925. Held's lively Jazz Age illustrations made him one of the era's most popular artists. RIGHT: Daniel Fitzpatrick, *St. Louis Post-Dispatch*, September 21, 1924. *"What we want in America is less government in business and more business in government," declared President Harding. Stocks soared and business boomed during the 1920s, thanks to the government's laissez-faire policies.*

Jay N. "Ding" Darling of the *Des Moines Register* had been cartooning since 1900, doing work that was light and amusing—reminiscent of another Midwesterner, the *Chicago Tribune*'s John McCutcheon. But World War I politicized Ding. As the death toll in Europe climbed, he spoke out against the isolationist position of those around him and even on his own paper. Editor and publisher Gardner Cowles watched as his cartoonist's work took on a decidedly independent point of view and to his credit maintained a hands-off policy. At war's end Ding was one of the few supporters of Woodrow Wilson's call for the United States to join the League of Nations, an organization for international co-operation established by the victorious Allied powers. His cartoons chronicled both the weary president's hopes as he crisscrossed the country trying to sell the League and its ultimate defeat at the hands of Congress in 1920. Richard West calls Ding's pro-League series "the best graphic defense of the League by an American." When Wilson died in 1924, Ding drew a memorial cartoon aptly named "That peace which was in life denied him." Like Wilson, he believed that without a peace organization another world war was inevitable.

THE LEAGUE OF NATIONS' ARGUMENT IN A NUTSHELL

Jay N. "Ding" Darling (1876-1962), *Des Moines Register*, circa 1919. *Darling lived in Des Moines, Iowa, but his cartoons were syndicated nationally by the New York Herald (later the Herald Tribune). His drawings appear to be done with a pen but were actually painted on large paper with a brush.*

Self-caricature, Jay N. "Ding" Darling.

"NOW, THEN, ALL TOGETHER: 'MY COUNTRY, 'TIS OF THEE!'"

LEFT: Joseph Keppler, *Puck*, July 3, 1889. RIGHT: Rollin Kirby, *New York World*, January 17, 1920. *Kirby's "Mr. Dry" had nineteenth-century antecedents in Joseph Keppler's "Old Man Prohibition."*

While discussion of the fate of the League dragged on, America enacted other legislation it had been dallying with for decades. The 18th and 19th Amendments passed practically in tandem in 1919 and 1920: one outlawed the sale or manufacture of intoxicating liquors; the other granted women the right to vote. Each was embraced wholeheartedly by the cartoonist community.

Rollin Kirby's "Mr. Dry" became the symbol of the Prohibition era. Like Joseph Keppler before him, he attacked the hypocrisy that put drinking behind closed doors. But his simplified cartoon style, eliminating all unnecessary details and often reducing the frame to a single symbolic figure, was a far cry from the elaborate vignettes of the Gilded Age and led the way in defining the look of the modern cartoon. Kirby won the first Pulitzer Prize for editorial cartooning in 1922 and was the first cartoonist to win three of the coveted awards (1925, 1929).

Historian Alice Sheppard has assembled the work of more than three dozen female cartoonists who published their prosuffrage cartoons primarily in women's magazines. "After the campaign succeeded these cartoons vanished from the printed page," noted Signe Wilkinson, one of contemporary America's few female cartoonists, "leaving rare, brittle clippings and the 19th Amendment as the only traces of their public lives."

Since the golden days of *Puck, Judge,* and *Life,* humor magazines had been fighting a losing battle against the daily newspapers. In 1917 *Puck* was taken over by Hearst, who killed it the next year and transplanted the famous *Puck* trademark onto the masthead of the *Journal*'s Sunday comic supplement. By 1920 *Judge* had stooped to soliciting one-liners called "Krazy Kracks" at five dollars a crack. *Life* had been taken over by Charles Dana Gibson, a better artist than publisher, and was limping along with trite cartoons.

Then, in 1925, the *New Yorker,* whose prospectus announced that it would be designed for the sophisticate rather than "the old lady of Dubuque," was founded by Harold Ross, who surrounded himself with some of the best talent in America. One of his first catches was art director Rea Irvin. Soon the accepted way to read the *New Yorker* was by starting with the cartoons, wrote Ross biographer Dale Kramer. The cartoons were directed at New York's well-heeled set. The artwork was fresh and the captions flippant.

The "old lady from Dubuque" Ross alluded to was the *Saturday Evening Post.* Bought as a failing periodical for $1,000 in 1897, the *Saturday Evening Post* by 1920 had become the most popular publication in America with a circulation of one million reaching an estimated five million readers. "To read the *Post* was to become American, to participate in the American experience," wrote Jay Cohn, biographer of *Post* editor George Lorimar. Each week brought articles, illustrations, and cartoons in which the nineteenth-century values of hard work and thrift were the driving themes. Norman Rockwell was the magazine's celebrated illustrator and Herbert Johnson its cartoonist. Johnson, who dressed like a banker in a three-piece suit complete with watch fob, told *Post* readers that he came to cartooning after stints

"MAKE WAY!"

Laura Foster, *Life*, October 10, 1912.
Foster was one of the few women to have her cartoons printed in mainstream publications such as Life.

ABOVE: Clifford Berryman (1869-1949), *Washington Star*, 1915.

RIGHT:
Clifford Berryman, *Washington Star*, 1928.

LEFT:
Self-caricature, Clifford Berryman, *Cartoon* magazine, June 1912.

Before Washington had "Herblock," they had Clifford Berryman, who worked for the Washington Star from 1908 to 1949 (and was followed by his son, James Berryman, who retired in 1965.) Although his statement was seldom confrontational, Berryman's craftsmanship was superb. His clean, stylized caricatures were sought-after mementos for senators, congressmen, and presidents. Berryman's first presidential caricature was of Theodore Roosevelt; he invented the Teddy bear. He would record the administrations of eight presidents, including those of Woodrow Wilson and Herbert Hoover.

LEFT: Herbert Johnson (1878-1956), *Saturday Evening Post*, 1928. RIGHT: Oliver Harrington, *New York State Contender*, October 22, 1932. *Many African American newspapers challenged their readers to abandon their traditional support of the Republican party and vote for Roosevelt.*

at clerking in a country store, stenography, and bookkeeping, and had had no formal art training when he began cartooning at age eighteen. His career read like a *Post* prototype, and his cartoons mirrored that shared perspective. Johnson's cartoon's were loose in style, filled with momentum, and decidedly funny.

Staunchly probusiness in its views, the magazine supported Republicans Warren Harding and Calvin Coolidge, but its favorite son was Herbert Hoover, secretary of commerce in the Coolidge administration. The *Post* brought the Stanford-educated engineer to the attention of the nation in a series of editorials supporting his candidacy in 1928. Called upon to support the magazine's stance, Johnson's cartoons during this period lack his normal gaiety and take on a somber, moralistic attitude.

President Hoover came into office just as the stock market was about to crash and would end up taking the blame for a decade of unregulated speculation and spending. His personal failure was an inability to judge the impact of the 1929 crash on the American psyche. Hoover's claims that "prosperity was just around the corner" fell on incredulous ears: one out of four farms was sold for taxes; 5,000 banks were closed; and, by 1933, there were fifteen million unemployed Americans. The Great Depression had arrived.

Franklin D. Roosevelt, who became president in 1933, called his administration the New Deal, and its programs exploded over the American landscape like a string of alphabetic firecrackers: CCC, AAA, NRA, WPA, and TVA. The president lashed out at the depression in all directions, and cartoonists lashed back at his policies. The majority of cartoonists were conservative. Herbert Johnson's anti-New Deal cartoons were typical of most cartoonists' attitudes. They whooped with a malicious glee, demonstrating their creator's antipathy toward FDR's new programs. Liberals also attacked the president's policies. William Cropper, who drew for socialist publications such as the New Masses and the Liberator, felt that Roosevelt's

Peter Arno (1904-68), unpublished *New Yorker* cover, 1932. *In this cover drawn for the New Yorker weeks before the actual inauguration, Peter Arno accurately foresaw the outcome of placing Herbert Hoover and Franklin Delano Roosevelt in the same limousine. A master caricaturist, Arno sets up the contrast between the two men, who had exchanged insults throughout the campaign. The cover was never published. After an assassination attempt on FDR in mid-February 1933, in which the mayor of Chicago was killed while riding in the president's car,* New Yorker *editors decided to use a less provocative cover.*

TROJAN HORSE AT OUR GATE

"I'VE GOT THE ENGINE STARTED, BUT..."

ABOVE: Carey Orr (1890-1967), *Chicago Tribune*, September 17, 1935. *Carey Orr worked alongside John McCutcheon and Joseph Parrish at the Chicago Tribune, once called "a kind of Yellowstone Park for the disappearing herd of cartoonists."*

ABOVE RIGHT: Herbert Johnson, *Saturday Evening Post*, 1935. *"The great confusion is epidemic,"* Herbert Johnson wrote in *the foreword to a book of his anti-New Deal cartoons. "It is not expected that a handful of cartoons will have any clarifying effect in the campaign ... but if they stimulate some sober thought upon matters of critical importance to the country, their author will be gratified."*

BOTTOM: Herbert Johnson, *Saturday Evening Post*, 1935.

programs were antilabor and courted the country's moneyed interests. Rollin Kirby, *New York World Telegram*, and Herbert Block, NEA Syndicate, showed their support for the humanitarianism evidenced in the New Deal. Jacob Burck's work for the *Daily Worker* was the only source of ongoing support. It was support the Roosevelt administration did not necessarily welcome.

Cartoonists may have hated Roosevelt's policies, but they loved the man. Like his fifth cousin, Teddy, FDR was frequently caricatured. His broad, confident smile punctuated by an ever-present cigarette holder always defiantly upturned, belied his crippled legs ravaged by polio. During the twelve years of his administration few cartoons were drawn that suggested the president's handicap.

The extreme hardship and personal suffering that surrounded the era was not a subject cartoonists could easily depict. Misery of that magnitude is hardly funny. Reginald Marsh, Boardman Robinson, and other artists who had earlier contributed to *The Masses,* sketched the makeshift existence of the unemployed. While these drawings were good, their attention to detail seems to diffuse rather than reinforce personal misery. It is the work of

THE SPHINX—1940 MODEL

ABOVE: Leo Joseph Roche, *Buffalo Courier Express*, November 16, 1939. *Roosevelt's refusal to state whether he would break tradition and run for a third term infuriated potential Democratic contenders.*

RIGHT: William Gropper (1897-1977), 1934. *Gropper transformed Roosevelt into Mae West, one of the most popular movie stars of the 1930s. Roosevelt uses West's famous beckoning call to invite Wall Street bankers, whose calling cards and portraits lay on the table.*

COME UP AND SEE ME SOMETIME

"I DO WISH SHE'D HURRY BACK"

"BUT IT WOULD MAKE SUCH A NICE SCOOP
IF YOU'D ONLY TELL ME, FRANKLIN,"

"GOSH MRS. ROOSEVELT,
IT SURE IS A SMALL WORLD!"

ABOVE LEFT: Jacob Burck (1904-82), *Minneapolis Times*, October 26, 1942.

ABOVE CENTER: Jacob Burck, *Chicago Times*, May 1940.

ABOVE RIGHT: Jacob Burck, September 1943. *Because of her outspokenness on issues and her commitment to causes (which she chronicled in a syndicated column), Eleanor Roosevelt was the first First Lady to be followed by journalists and cartoonists. Mrs. Roosevelt's busy travel schedule and her habit of popping up everywhere were constant sources of amusement.*

BELOW RIGHT: Jack Ohman, *Oregonian*, 1994. *Cartoonists set their sights on First Lady Hillary Rodham Clinton from the moment her husband announced his candidacy for president in 1991. She was attacked for her name, her hairstyles, her aggressive personality, her leading role in crafting health care policy—and her disavowal of culinary pursuits.*

LEFT: John McCutcheon, *Chicago Tribune*, August 19, 1931. *McCutcheon comments on the wave of bank failures that crippled the nation during the 1930s, using the squirrel as a symbol of prudence. The cartoon won the 1932 Pulitzer Prize.*

ABOVE: Reginald Marsh (1898-1954), 1932.

WPA photographers that best captures the desperation of the 1930s.

In Harlem, Roosevelt and his New Deal were seen from yet another perspective. Although most African Americans had clung to Hoover and the Republican Party of Abraham Lincoln, a new generation saw hope in Roosevelt's promises. Mainstream papers in segregated America paid little attention to the black communities that had grown in many northern cities. But an independent black press flourished, and papers like the *Chicago Defender*, *Pittsburgh Courier*, and New York's *Amsterdam News* found their way by rail to every city with a large black population.

Spurred by the Harlem Renaissance of the 1920s, African American artists grew confident and began to counter a century of demeaning stereotypes with their own characterizations. "Bootsie," a well-meaning ne'er-do-well who was the embodiment of Harlem's fads and foibles, was created by Oliver Harrington in 1936. The young artist's work and that of other black political cartoonists like the *Amsterdam News'* William Chase were equally insightful, speaking out against lynchings, forced segregation, and job discrimination. For many Americans, "Ollie" provided their first cartoon voice. The poet Langston Hughes declared Harrington "Negro America's favorite cartoonist."

Edmund Duffy was one of the few white cartoonists to speak out against racial injustice.

When Duffy joined the *Baltimore Sun* in 1924, it was dominated by the larger-than-life personality of H. L. Mencken, one of this century's finest editors. "Give me a good cartoonist," said Mencken, "and I can throw out half the editorial staff." Duffy and Mencken hit it off; for the next twenty-five years, they would produce blistering attacks on issues aimed at all levels of government. Duffy targeted the Ku Klux Klan, which had become a major force in American politics. In one cartoon he unmasked a Klansman, revealing a dull-witted weakling, who became completely powerless without his robe.

Maryland was a state steeped in racial unrest. In 1931 a mob lynched an African American accused of murdering a white businessman. Duffy condemned the event with brilliant juxtaposition, captioning his cartoon with "Maryland, My Maryland," the state anthem. The cartoon created a greater furor than the event itself. "Outrage was immediate and directed at the wicked cartoonist Duffy, Mencken and the Sunpapers," wrote Harold Williams in his book on the *Baltimore Sun.* "Unruly street demonstrations erupted, and the newspapers delivery vans were ambushed and drivers beaten." "The cartoon represented Duffy at his best: an uncompromising assertion of the world as he saw it," said his biographer, S. L. Harrison. Duffy would win his first (of three) Pulitzer Prizes that year, but not for that cartoon.

The Pulitzer Prize has often been given to the right person for the wrong reason. By and large the judges have honored those drawings that avoided the specific and the controversial. Neither

"PUT IT ON AGAIN!"

ABOVE: Edmund Duffy (1899-1962), *Baltimore Sun*, December 6, 1931. *The last notable cartoonist from Baltimore had been Adalbert Volck who took the side of the South during the Civil War.*

LEFT: Edmund Duffy, *Baltimore Sun*, January 23, 1928.

C. D. Batchelor (1888-1977), *New York Daily News*, April 25, 1936. ***The skeleton as a symbol for death returns predictably as each new war looms on the horizon, but Batchelor's Pulitzer Prize-winning cartoon goes beyond a hackneyed rendition, turning war into a prostitute beckoning European youth and suggesting (by omission) that the United States would not be taken in by the invitation.***

Duffy's Klansman nor Kirby's "Mr. Dry" were ever recognized by the Pulitzer committee. In 1932 John McCutcheon, by now America's most beloved cartoonist, won his first Pulitzer Prize as much for his contribution to cartooning as for a cartoon on bank failures, "A Wise Economist Asks a Question." By decade's end, cartoons on war would capture the Pulitzer award. C. D. Batchelor's provocative cartoon "Come on in ... I Used to Know Your Daddy," one of the most insightful for which the prize has been given, is as forceful today as it was with the rise of fascism in 1936, when Spain's General Franco joined Italy's Mussolini and Germany's Hitler in turning Europe into an armed camp.

As war spread across Europe, Americans threw on their isolationist cloak once more. "We are not isolationists," said Roosevelt, "except insofar as we seek to isolate ourselves completely from war." Rather than portray Adolf Hitler as the terrifying would-be conqueror that he was, cartoonists were more apt to turn him into a comic figure—a quack, the village idiot, or just that little man with the funny mustache.

One artist drew from a more prescient view: Daniel Fitzpatrick at the *St. Louis Post-*

"AH! THOSE WERE THE GOOD OLD DAYS."

HIROSHIMA

LEFT: Vaughn Shoemaker, Chicago Daily News, September 8, 1938. Field Marshal Herman Göring called Shoemaker's work "horrible examples of anti-Nazi propaganda." CENTER: Edwin Marcus (1885-1961), New York Times, August 5, 1945. RIGHT: Robert Osborn (1904-94), 1945. Osborn's stark depiction of the atomic bomb at Hiroshima underscored the fear and horror that unleashing the tremendous power of the atom brought.

Dispatch. By setting the Nazi swastika in motion as a machine of death, he delivered one of the most significant symbols of World War II (see page 13). Fitzpatrick's style was reminiscent of his predecessor Robert Minor's powerful crayon approach. Although his early cartoons often contained human figures, as his style evolved Fitzpatrick began to frequently omit them altogether. Stark, precise symbols became his calling card. In reducing major, cataclysmic events to two-dimensional abstract representation, Fitzpatrick has yet to be surpassed.

Japan's attack on Pearl Harbor brought the United States into the war. Where Hitler had become the symbol of German aggression, cartoonists demonized the Japanese by creating vicious but generalized characters.

Sgt. Bill Mauldin showed the people back home what war looked like from a foxhole in the series he drew for the *49th Division News* and later, *Stars and Stripes.* These were not patriotic tableaux of valor as had been laboriously engraved for *Harper's* front pages during the Civil War or for the Bureau of Cartoons during World War I. These were the day-to-day frustrations of Willie and Joe, two bedraggled

Self-caricature, Bill Mauldin, *What's Got Your Back Up*, 1961.

Bill Mauldin, *Stars and Stripes*, June 1, 1944.

Bill Mauldin, United Feature Syndicate, 1946.

soldiers serving on the front lines, who each day belied any thought that war is noble.

When Mauldin joined the army in 1940 he was nineteen years old. "I drew pictures for and about the dogfaces because I knew what their life was like and I understood their gripes. I wanted to make something out of the humorous situations which come up even when you don't think life could be any more miserable." Willie and Joe earned the antagonism of General George Patton and the adoration of his troops. At war's end Willie appeared on the cover of Time magazine. Mauldin became the youngest cartoonist ever to win a Pulitzer Prize and returned home to enormous popularity and lucrative syndication offers.

Mauldin called it as he saw it during the war and won praise and prizes. The same approach to events back home, however, did not sell well. America was booming again and looked pretty good to those who had survived a world war and a depression. At first Mauldin focused his attention on the plight of the returning GI. Soon his commentary expanded to issues of racism, the Cold War, and the House Un-American Activities Committee, which had been probing subversive activities

"BLOODSTAINS AGAIN!"

Bill Mauldin, United Feature Syndicate, 1946.

"INVESTIGATE THEM? HECK, THAT'S MAH POSSE."

Bill Mauldin, United Feature Syndicate, 1947.

FREEDOM'S BRAVE SENTINELS

Bill Mauldin, United Feature Syndicate, 1946.

since the 1930s. Editors who had bought Mauldin's series for entertainment now found themselves printing cartoons filled with controversy. Cancellations began pouring in. Mauldin wrote, "It was explained to me by the syndicate, in a tone reserved for backward children and young men with stirrings of a social conscience, that selling cartoons on a nation-wide basis was big business and that it was damn poor business I was doing." Syndication was now a major factor in the business of cartoons. It gave people in small towns across America a chance to laugh at the work of America's best cartoonists. But it was the syndicates that selected which cartoonists and cartoons would be seen, and in demanding that cartoons appeal to the widest cross section of America, a homogeneity of style and approach was created that undermined the essence of cartooning: a unique point of view.

Mauldin's series of drawings condemning the hypocrisy he saw around him in the United States upon his return home may well be among his best work. But his syndicate didn't want to run the cartoons and his audience didn't want to hear their message. Frustrated, Mauldin left cartooning temporarily, in 1949.

THE CARTOONIST VERSUS THE TELEVISION: 1947 - 1974

ASK BABY BOOMERS ABOUT growing up and they might tell you about crouching under school desks, home bomb-shelters, and Sputnik. The 1950s fanned fears of Cold War confrontation. They also engendered cynicism. Playing counterpoint to "I Like Ike," the first campaign slogan many boomers cut their teeth on *Mad,* a humor magazine that titillated the postwar generation's acerbic wit. Television became a major fixture in every household; there was Howdy Doody, *Dragnet,* Ed Sullivan, and the nightly news. And the news was not good. As the 1950s became the 1960s, bad news took the form of Castro and the Bay of Pigs, the assassination of President Kennedy in Dallas, the escalating war in Vietnam. The changing times witnessed a pervasive listlessness in the ranks of American cartooning. New energy and new approaches would be needed if the political cartoon was to continue as a force for change in the television age.

In Washington, D.C., however, there existed a remarkable source of cartooning energy. For sheer impact, a nation's capital is the ideal place for a political cartoonist, and as cartoonist on the only morning paper in Washington, Herbert L. Block (better known as Herblock) had enjoyed a special breakfast-table relationship with presidents, cabinet officers, members of Congress, the diplomatic corps, and Supreme Court justices, as well as national reporters. He had been cartooning for newspa-

EVERYONE IS A LITTLE SUBVERSIVE BUT THEE AND ME, AND SOMETIMES I THINK EVEN THEE—,"

"SO MUCH FOR CHEATING. NOW FOR A NICE, SADISTIC WESTERN."

EFT: Daniel Fitzpatrick, *St. Louis Post-Dispatch*, February 23, 1947.
GHT: Bill Mauldin, *St. Louis Post-Dispatch*, November 3, 1959.

pers since 1929, and had won a Pulitzer Prize in 1942 while working for the Newspaper Enterprise Association, a syndication service. But Block would not reach full stride until joining the *Washington Post* in 1946. Washington had never before had such an independent-minded cartoonist sitting on its front porch.

Block's distinct point of view, given free rein by his paper, established him as a pull-no-punches cartoonist. He conveyed the public's fears of the atomic bomb through a menacing character called "Mr. Atom." He correctly saw the civil rights of the nation's black population as the next big agenda item. He even attacked the Daughters of the American Revolution for discrimination. But Block was to show the courage of his convictions when he chose to confront an issue that many other cartoonists—and their papers—gave a wide berth, by aiming his sights at the junior U.S. senator from Wisconsin, Joseph McCarthy.

In a speech given to a West Virginia women's club in February 1950, McCarthy

FIRE!

Herbert Block, *Washington Post*, June 17, 1949.

THE VERDICT

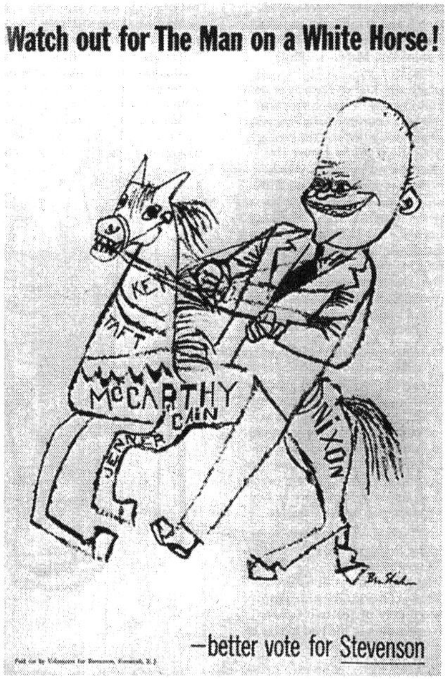

ABOVE: Joseph Parrish (1905-89), *Chicago Tribune*, 1955.

ABOVE RIGHT: Daniel Fitzpatrick, *St. Louis Post-Dispatch*, November 5, 1952.

RIGHT: Ben Shahn (1889-1969), Democratic campaign poster, 1952.

LEFT: Herbert Block, *Washington Post*, March 29, 1950. RIGHT: Herbert Block, *Washington Post*, March 4, 1954.

waved a piece of paper and claimed to have the names of 205 "card-carrying" Communists who were employed by the State Department. The speech set off an unprincipled, publicity-grabbing hunt for domestic Communists and "fellow-travelers" that would last for four years. The malicious crusade gave the country a bad case of the shakes and the lexicographers a new word—"McCarthyism," coined by none other than Herbert Block.

In the midst of Joseph McCarthy's witch hunt, General Dwight D. Eisenhower was elected with a landslide majority in 1952. Ike and Mamie were embraced by a sentimental public that treated them like a favorite aunt and uncle. All hoped that World War II's most famous general would help curb the fears that beset the nation as Russian aggression abroad and McCarthy's campaign at home continued to grow.

Walt Kelley, creator of the comic strip "Pogo," joined Block and the few other satirists willing to stand up to McCarthy's televised investigations and in the process influenced many young cartoonists. "Walt Kelley put rage back into the political cartoon—something that had been missing since the early days of the trust-buster cartoons in the early 20th century," Jules Feiffer recalled. "He brought a kind of moral indignation to the form, pure and with a degree of zealotry that I admire." Senator Simple J. Malarkey, a dead ringer

Walt Kelly (1913-73), *Pogo*, Hall Syndicate, May 7, 1953.

for Joe McCarthy, made his first appearance in Pogo's swamp universe in May 1953. Newspapers responded unfavorably to Kelly's outspokenness, dropping selected strips or canceling the feature entirely. Kelly wrote about a run-in with the *Providence Journal,* which threatened to ban "Pogo" if Malarkey's face appeared again (even though the *Journal* was opposed to Senator McCarthy). "Politics has no place in the comic pages," its editors explained. "Miss Bombah," a Rhode Island red chicken, had already appeared in "Pogo." Shortly after the paper's editorial, Kelly identified Bombah as coming from Providence. When Malarkey sees her approach, he quickly covers his face with a bag. The bag stayed in place until the *Journal* capitulated and reinstated "Pogo." In later years, Kelly would bring other figures from the news pages to the comic pages: a pig resembling Nikita Krushchev and a goat that bore a remarkable likeness to Fidel Castro.

Investigations on Capitol Hill sidetracked or destroyed the careers of many innocent people in the early 1950s. Jacob Burck, who had worked for *The Daily Worker* was targeted, but charges against him were dropped eventually. Ollie Harrington, a cartoonist for African American papers, was not as fortunate. After the war Harrington put aside drawing his popular cartoon feature, "Bootsie," to set up the public relations department of the NAACP. He spoke out against segregation and the treatment of the returning black soldier. In 1951 Harrington was notified by a friend that he was being investigated by the House Un-American Activities Committee and was advised to go to Europe, according to Thomas Inge, Harrington's biographer. The cartoonist's most memorable work on life in Harlem and the black struggle for civil equality would be penned over his forty years as an expatriate in Europe and sent home to papers like the *Chicago Defender* and *Pittsburgh Courier.*

When it came to civil rights, Eisenhower

"GENERAL BLOTCHIT, YOU TAKE YOUR TANKS AND FEINT AT LYNCHVILLE,"

ABOVE: Oliver Harrington, *Bootsie and Others*, 1958.

ABOVE RIGHT: Clifford Baldowski (1917-99), *Atlanta Constitution*, December 12, 1957.

BELOW RIGHT: Paul Conrad, *Denver Post*, September 26, 1957.

"KEEP YOUR EYE ON THE CRYSTAL BALL!"

"... NUTS ...!"

The early civil rights struggles in the South, particularly the desegregation of schools, found few cartoonists willing to confront the sensitive issues at hand. These three cartoons, drawn from different view-points, are exceptions. The confrontation between Arkansas' Governor Orval Faubus and Federal troops called in to ensure the entry of black stu-dents to Little Rock's Central High School was the first of many such incidents.

Duncan Macpherson (1924-93), *Toronto Star*, 1960.
Cartoonists like Macpherson, one of Canada's best, often focused on events in the United States.

and cartoonists trod timidly. But the 1954 Supreme Court decision *Brown* v. *Board of Education* would force the nation to reevaluate the first of its long-standing Jim Crow laws: segregation of public schools. Over the next decade most cartoonists avoided the long and protracted drama unfolding in the South. The confrontation between National Guardsmen and parents of white children in Little Rock, Arkansas, and Rosa Parks' refusal to give up her seat to a white passenger on a Montgomery, Alabama, bus in 1955 were covered with tired cliches of ringing bells labeled "civil rights," bearing captions such as "Let freedom ring." Yet the year-long boycott of city buses by Montgomery's African Americans would help bring down another Jim Crow policy and elevate Parks' minister, Martin Luther King Jr., to national recognition.

Caricatures of King, Malcolm X, and the other African American leaders who rose to prominence during this period are hard to find. Cartoonists and their newspapers grew so sensitive to the volatility of caricaturing black leaders, fearing that they would be perceived as racial slurs and thereby bring resentment from the black community, that they shied away from any depiction whatsoever. Instead, cartoonists employed generic situations and peopled them with generic black figures. Martin Luther King Jr. became an invisible man in the cartoons of an era in which he was a prominent player.

The race for the White House in 1960 between Eisenhower's vice president Richard Nixon and Massachusetts Senator John F. Kennedy was determined by a series of televised debates. According to polls, Kennedy, who was less well known, won the debates. He squeaked into office with a plurality of less than half of one percent of the vote, bringing a charming wife and his whole clan with him. Most cartoonists were fans of the new president. Their depictions of Kennedy were flattering, even reverential, and utterly boring as cartoons and caricatures.

Television brought foreign faces to the dinner tables of America, and here cartoonists didn't hold back. Soviet Premier Nikita Krushchev banging his shoe at the United Nations and Cuban Premier Fidel Castro sporting army fatigues and cigar were larger-than-life leaders who offered self-made caricatures.

Assassinated before the impact of his presidency could be fully realized, Kennedy's long-term treatment by the cartoonists will never be known. Many cartoonists continue to

"THIS PROGRAM IS COMING TO YOU LIVE"

"YOU CAN HAVE THEM, THEY'RE NO GOOD ANYHOW"

ABOVE LEFT: Jim Ivey, *San Francisco Examiner, 1960. The whole world watched as Nixon and Kennedy sparred in the first televised presidential debates.*

BELOW LEFT: Gibson Crockett (1912-2000), *Washington Star,* November 21, 1962. *The Cuban Missle Crisis inspired this cartoon by "Gib" Crockett who joined Clifford Berryman and his son, Jim, at the Washington Star in 1933.*

ABOVE: Siegel/Drucker, *Mad,* December 1961. *Mad used familiar tunes to parody political topics, a device that became a popular feature in the magazine. Here, the Gilbert & Sullivan operetta HMS Pinafore provides the melody for Mad's commentary on the telegenic first family.*

LEFT: Bill Mauldin, *Chicago Sun-Times*, November 23, 1963. RIGHT: Bill Mauldin, *Chicago Sun-Times*, September 16, 1962.

omit cartoons on Kennedy from their published anthologies out of respect for his memory. Bill Mauldin's obituary cartoon captured the nation's grief at the young president's death and became one of the most famous cartoons in American history.

Mauldin, after a decade-long hiatus during which he went to Hollywood, learned to fly, and even ran for Congress from New York State, returned to cartooning in 1958, sitting down at the drawing board vacated by retiring *St. Louis Post-Dispatch* cartoonist Daniel Fitzpatrick. Four years later, having won a second Pulitzer Prize, he moved to the *Chicago Sun-Times,* where he would share editorial cartoonist responsibilities with another Pulitzer Prize winner, Jacob Burck.

While Mauldin ridiculed the southern redneck as the civil rights struggle turned from peaceful sit-ins to violent confrontations in the 1960s, a cartoonist and playwright from New York named Jules Feiffer probed the rhetoric and psychology of northern white liberals, finding contradictions that went to the very depths of the race issue. Feiffer's panels in the *Village Voice* read like mini-plays; they were not quite comic strips, but neither were they editorial cartoons. There could be no doubt, however, about their political volatility. Where Kelly had used the Okefenokee swamp as a metaphor for current events, Feiffer hit political reality head-on.

In his early cartoons, Feiffer often focused on the man-on-the-street to explain the political, social, and cultural undercurrents he saw about him. Each week his characters pondered the incongruities of life and politics, using carefully honed soliloquies that evolved through a series of four to eight drawings within a single panel. The inner-monologue style became Feiffer's trademark, and he would use it with blistering effect as he turned his sights on known political figures. Using sequential drawings and soliloquies was soon copied by others, and Feiffer's style is now a standard format in political cartoons. Underground and alternative publications have traditionally offered artists the opportunity to explore new styles and ideologies. Feiffer's fresh approach and sustained political vision gave the moribund craft of cartooning a much-needed kick in the pants.

Political cartooning in the mainstream press had become largely gag oriented and predictable during the 1950s. It seemed as though cartoonists had just run out of ideas. After the retirement of editorial cartoonist Edwin Marcus in 1958, the *New York Times* elected not to hire a replacement and later began commissioning artwork to illustrate its op-ed page.

Pat Oliphant arrived in the United States in 1964 from Australia to work for the *Denver Post.* "When I came here, it was during the Johnson-Goldwater [presidential] campaign. The place was alive with debate. I thought I had died and gone to heaven," Oliphant said.

Jules Feiffer, *Village Voice*, September 8, 1963.

THE VICTIMS

ABOVE:
Pat Oliphant, *Denver Post*, July 27, 1967.

RIGHT:
Pat Oliphant, *Denver Post*, August 2, 1967.

"I'm afraid to say, American cartooning was a laughingstock among other cartoonists in the world. All we ever saw was the Peace Dove with the scroll in its mouth, Hope coming over the hill, and the Rocky Road to prosperity. There was a stagnation one could see. Here was an audience that was really ready for a variety of new approaches." Like Feiffer, Oliphant steered away from worn-out symbolism and from relying on familiar political figures. Unlike Feiffer, who was—and is—an unabashed liberal, Oliphant's stand on an issue was not as predictable. His style was refreshing, exuberant, and unforgiving.

While most American-born cartoonists seemed to cower from hitting the headline-grabbing issue of civil rights head-on, Oliphant attacked it squarely, calling each incident as he saw it. In one cartoon, penned during rioting that broke out in the summer of 1967, he showed African Americans as victims of the lawlessness and looting within their own society. Two cartoons on the police, who were increasingly being called on to quell civil disturbances, show the cartoonist's contrasting points of view. In the first cartoon, the police are protagonists; in the next they are—almost—victims. Oliphant would make many more tough calls as he settled into dissecting his new society. A penguin named "Punk" appears in most of the Australian's work. Although Oliphant was not the first to use an alter-ego character to deliver his own commentary or a punch line, he made more consistent and better use of the technique than cartoonists before him. Punk was born when Oliphant was still living in Australia and worked for a conservative paper, the Advertiser in Adelaide. A friend had brought a penguin home in his knapsack from a trip. "It was an appealing little feller, and I incorporated it in a couple of cartoons I was doing," Oliphant explained. "It took off. People liked it and wanted to see more. Punk's continued use in my work after his initial good reception was far from a gimmick." As a young cartoonist, Oliphant had to fight to have his point of view represented. The penguin gave him a chance to add his own voice to the daily cartoons which were, as Oliphant describes it, "beaten out on a committee anvil somewhere around three p.m. every day by a group of editors of differing degrees of dullness, at a gathering called The Editorial Conference. I would leave these sessions in varying states of desperation and despair. Punk saved me from this. I could at least feel that a small

"I FORGET MAYOR DALEY'S ORDERS—ARE THESE 'SHOOT TO KILL' OR "MAIM AND CRIPPLE'?"

ABOVE: Pat Oliphant, *Denver Post*, June 17, 1968.

LEFT: Pat Oliphant, *Denver Post*, August 25, 1970.

corner of the cartoon was mine. I think it gave me the confidence to continue." Many other cartoonists now use similar alter-ego characters.

The baby boomers hit college in the 1960s, infused with the cynicism that Mad magazine had instilled and Feiffer and Oliphant now reinforced. For some, high school had been a training ground for nonviolent civil rights protests; college would unleash a more aggressive behavior as the focus on campuses turned to Vietnam. Lyndon Johnson, who had won the admiration of many for his aggressive civil rights stand, became suspect when, after campaigning as a "peace" president, he started bombing North Vietnam soon after the election. As student demonstrations grew in size, engulfing campus after campus in protest, the cartoonist community mirrored the conflicting points of view that divided the country as a whole.

The Vietnam War marked a turning point in editorial cartooning in the United States because it was the first time mainstream cartoonists consistently spoke out against their

Jules Feiffer, *Village Voice*, January 1, 1967.

Al Capp (1909-1979), *L'il Abner, Chicago Tribune/New York News Syndicate,* November 13, 1965. *In 1967 Al Capp attacked the Vietnam peace marchers as "SWINE" (Students Wildly Indignant about Nearly Everything) in his popular strip L'il Abner. He told a* Boston Globe *reporter, "The independent humorist has one function and this is to attack lunacy. He attacks it wherever it is. Now for 30 years I attacked lunacy on the Right because that's where it was.... If it shifts from Right to Left, as it did, I simply turn my aim."*

government's policy on the issue of war. The best cartoons were directed at President Johnson, who feared history's judgment if he became the first American president to lose one. Paul Szep's cartoon on Lyndon Johnson captured the personal hell the president had created for himself. Szep, a Canadian, had recently been hired by the *Boston Globe,* one of the first papers to come out against the war. Looking back on those early days, Szep remembered, "My ex-wife's father was a two-star general in the Canadian military and he had really sold me a bill of goods on Vietnam. I became aware that I had been lied to—deceived—and my cartoons reflected that." Szep created many passionate indictments of American policy in Vietnam.

Some of the best material on the Vietnam War would come from a group of artists whose chilling work crossed from illustration into political commentary. The *New York Review of Books* would bring the talents of caricaturist David Levine to national attention. As his famous portrait of Lyndon Johnson with the scar in the shape of Vietnam revealed, Levine had a genius for what *New York Times* art director Steven Heller described as "pinpointing a benign physical feature and metamorphosing it into a fatal character flaw." British cartoonist Ralph Steadman's work for *Rolling Stone* sounded a wake-up call to his American counterparts. It was matched by Edward Sorel, who freelanced at *Ramparts, Esquire,* and *Atlantic.* Not since the nineteenth century had such fine penmanship been tied to such blistering points of view.

BELOW: John Fischetti (1916-80), Publishers' Newspaper Syndicate, June 14, 1967.

RIGHT: Paul Szep, *Boston Globe*, 1960s.

BELOW RIGHT: Draper Hill, *Worcester Telegram*, May 3, 1968.

"SUNRISE....ALL THE FOREIGN TROUBLE MAKERS GOIN' TO SLEEP AN' ALL THE DOMESTIC ONES WAKIN' UP"

Paul Szep, *Boston Globe*, January 28, 1973. *Szep penned his impression of America's involvement in Vietnam in 1973. Little did he know that the final evacuation of U.S. personnel from the U.S. Embassy in Saigon would be accomplished by a desperate helicopter airlift of its inhabitants from atop the building. When this happened in April 1975,* The Boston Globe *reran Szep's cartoon, proving that history sometimes follows cartoons.*

PEACE OFFENSIVE

Edward Sorel, *Vista*, 1972.

The Democratic convention in Chicago nominated Vice President Hubert Humphrey as the party's choice in 1968. Try as he might, Humphrey could not disentangle himself from Johnson's policy calling for continued fighting in Vietnam, and the Democratic Party began to unravel in front of prime-time cameras. Television viewers were shocked when the screen cut from the confrontation on the convention floor to the confrontation between Mayor Richard Daley's police and demonstrators protesting the ongoing Vietnam War.

Three months later, the American people chose Richard Nixon as the next president. Like Tweed in the 1870s, Nixon provided many of the natural ingredients for good caricature: the narrow, sloping shoulders, the five-o'clock shadow, the heavy jowls, the beady eyes, the ski-jump nose. "If Richard Nixon hadn't existed," said historian Roger Fischer, "cartoonists would have had to invent him. Never had nature so perfectly molded physiognomy to personality." Herblock and Richard Nixon had arrived in Washington the same year, 1947. By 1954 Nixon's red-baiting had so incensed Block that he drew a picture of the vice president climbing out of the sewer. Later he chose to always represent Nixon with a swarthy five-o'clock shadow. In an October 1958 press conference in Minneapolis, Nixon commented on the hardships of public figures and their families. He was not complaining for himself, he said, but it was "difficult when your ten-year-old daughter comes home from school and says her classmates are teasing her about a cartoon in the morning paper." Two years later, when he was the Republican presidential nominee, Nixon reportedly asserted, "I have to erase the Herblock image."

LEFT: Paul Szep, *Boston Globe*, August 30, 1968. RIGHT: Jules Feiffer, *Village Voice*, June 4, 1972.

"HERE HE COMES NOW"

"STRANGE THEY ALL SEEM TO HAVE SOME CONNECTION WITH THIS PLACE."

LEFT: Herbert Block, *Washington Post*, October 29, 1954. CENTER: Herbert Block, *Washington Post*, November 7, 1968. RIGHT: Herbert Block, *Washington Post*, June 23, 1972.

Once Nixon was elected in 1968, Block's editors asked him to consider giving his old adversary a new image. *Washington Post* editor Russell Wiggins sent Block a razor with a poem that closed with the lines:

> *... join the good and kind and true*
> *The faithful, just and brave,*
> *And grasp this razor in your hand,*
> *And give that man a shave.*

Herblock agreed to the shave. Shortly before Nixon's reelection in 1972, a break-in at the Democratic National Committee headquarters produced a scandal of major proportions. Herblock sensed a connection to the White House. He was not alone.

One of the most powerful series of cartoons on the Watergate scandal would come from California, Nixon's home state. Paul Conrad had risen to prominence in American cartooning over the past two decades, working first for the *Denver Post* and then joining the *Los Angeles Times* in 1964. His views are so fiercely presented that his colleague Doug Marlette wrote, "Conrad's 20/20 insight stands him squarely in the tradition of Old Testament prophets. If Jeremiah had drawn, he would have drawn like Conrad." Besides

"AS PRESIDENT, JERRY, YOU COULD GRANT ME CLEMENCY ... BUT, IT WOULD BE WRONG!"

HIS OWN WORST ENEMY

"ALAS, POOR AGNEW, MITCHELL, STANS, EHRLICHMAN, HALDEMAN, DEAN, KALMBACH, LARUE, MARDIAN, STRACHAN, MCCORD, LIDDY, CHAPIN, HUNT, COLSON, KROGH, MAGRUDER, YOUNG—I KNEW THEM ..."

INSIDE H. R. HALDEMAN

ABOVE: Pat Oliphant,
***Denver Post*, August 1, 1973.**
FAR RIGHT: Pat Oliphant, 1984.
Ten years after Nixon's resignation, Oliphant created this lithograph of him.
RIGHT: Herbert Block,
***Washington Post*,**
May 24, 1974.

OPPOSITE PAGE, ABOVE LEFT:
Paul Conrad, *Los Angeles Times*,
August 8, 1974.
BELOW LEFT: Paul Conrad,
***Los Angeles Times*, July 1, 1973.**
RIGHT: Paul Conrad,
***Los Angeles Times*,**
October 17, 1973.

Tony Auth, *Philadelphia Inquirer*, February 20, 1974.

Mike Peters, *Dayton Daily News*, 1973.

Doug Marlette, *Charlotte Observer*, November 30, 1973. ***Many cartoons done following the Watergate break-in focused on tapes recorded of every conversation in the Oval Office. Nixon's secretary, Rose Mary Woods, was asked to demonstrate to the court how she had accidentally erased a key section of one tape.***

Jeff MacNelly (1947-2000), *Richmond News Leader*, 1973. ***President Nixon refused to release the tapes he had secretly recorded until Federal Judge John Sirica ordered the White House to turn them over to determine if they had been altered.***

Garry Trudeau, *Doonesbury*, Universal Press Syndicate, May 29, 1973. ***Trudeau's most contentious strip during the Nixon era may have been this cartoon on Attorney General John Mitchell, then under indictment for his role in the Watergate cover-up. Dozens of papers refused to run the cartoon. A*** **Washington Post** ***editorial stated, "If anyone is going to find any defendant guilty, it's going to be the due process of justice, not a comic strip artist. We cannot have one standard for the news pages and another for the comics."***

three Pulitzer Prizes, Conrad had the honor of being the only cartoonist on Nixon's "enemies list," the subject of many cartoons. Conrad drew more than a hundred cartoons on Watergate between 1972 and 1974. His work sparkled with artistry, daring, and imagination in both concept and execution. Conrad's versatile styles and diverse imagery were breathtaking, making dramatic use of silhouette, scratchboard, and literary allusion.

A new generation had taken to the drawing boards by the early 1970s. Many had worked on their college papers: Tony Auth at UCLA; Jeff MacNelly at the University of North Carolina; Doug Marlette at Florida State University; Mike Peters at Washington University; and Garry Trudeau at Yale. When Marlette went before the local draft board to explain why he should be granted conscientious-objector status, he showed the political cartoons he had drawn for Florida State's daily newspaper, the *Flambeau.* His request was granted.

Cartoons had been pivotal in deciding the presidential contest between Grover Cleveland and James Blaine in 1884, but by 1968 television had come to dominate the public's perception of events. Yet in the cartoons on Watergate and the presidency of Richard Nixon, cartoonists unleashed a dazzling variety of their visual arsenal. A golden age of cartooning had returned.

COMING FULL CIRCLE: 1975 - 1996

THINK OF ALL THE NEWS EVENTS that have paraded across the television screen since the days of Watergate and Vietnam. We have been assaulted by imagery and pummeled by unsolicited information. There have been oil crises and hostage crises; the *Challenger* and Chernobyl; the fall of the Berlin Wall and the rise of Nelson Mandela; man's assault on the environment and his fellow man; Solidarity and Tiananmen Square; Desert Storm and Bosnia; O.J. Simpson and Newt Gingrich. Television has created indelible visual images of each of these events and personalities that linger in viewers' minds in long shots, medium shots, and close-ups. Cartoonists have only one lens, the lens of satire, and they have discovered that it is difficult trying to make sense out of the confusion and cacophony that surrounds our daily lives. "I was a lot more sage in the '50s and '60s," said Jules Feiffer. "I knew absolutely what needed to be said about the Cold War, Nixon, Johnson, Kennedy and Eisenhower. Everything seemed decipherable and measurable. Now we seem to be in free fall." America, once the young kid on the block, was creeping into middle age, and toting all the baggage of its two hundred years. It was now the unquestioned leader of the world. But to sustain that position, its bureaucracy and budget had taken on a life of their own. A profound cynicism began to stir within the nation and among cartoonists.

"HURRY IT UP, WILL YOU, NOAH?"

Pat Oliphant, *Denver Post*, November 3, 1974.

Pat Oliphant changed newspapers in 1975, moving from the *Denver Post* to the *Washington Star.* Now, two of America's most influential cartoonists, Oliphant and Herblock, resided in the nation's capital. Together with Paul Conrad, they remained the most important and consistent political cartoonists working in daily newspapers in the United States.

New trends, styles, and outside influences would reveal themselves over the next twenty years, as cartoonists now lobbed their missiles at five successive administrations. When Gerald Ford became president in 1974, they captured the nation's hope that he could bring the country together again and delighted in his physical malaprops. They shared Jimmy Carter's triumph in negotiating a peace treaty between Egypt and Israel in 1979, and his humiliation later that year as Iran fell under the control of the Ayatollah Khomeini and fifty-two hostages were held in the U.S. Embassy in Tehran. Not only were the Americans in Iran held hostage, so, too, was the entire nation.

Paul Conrad, *Los Angeles Times*, December 1, 1978.

LEFT: Mike Peters, *Dayton Daily News*, November 3, 1976. *Jimmy Carter's wide smile kept cartoonists busy. Only the president's brother, Billy, received more attention. Billy's antics were tolerated until it was discovered that he had accepted money to lobby on behalf of the Libyan government.* RIGHT: Doug Marlette, *Charlotte Observer*, 1980.

Ronald Reagan's landslide victory in 1980 put Jeff MacNelly, one of the few cartoonists to look at issues from a conservative perspective, in a new situation. His views were now in step with the party in the White House, and he wasn't sure he liked it. "Reagan rode into town like the sheriff. So early on I drew him as a cowboy," MacNelly remembered. "He had an agenda, and I was behind him. That was hard for me because I hate to do cheerleading cartoons. I've been screaming for somebody for fifteen years and suddenly he gets elected. That's great, but what do I do? I can't go around saying, 'Gee, isn't the president doing a great job?' That's not what a political cartoonist does. So I had my problems with Reagan early on."

MacNelly's rise in the world of political cartooning had been meteoric. Although he worked for a small paper, the *Richmond News Leader,* his political cartoons were carried in hundreds of papers. In 1972, after only nineteen months as a cartoonist, he was awarded his first Pulitzer Prize. (He would win two more, in 1978 and 1985.) Five months after Reagan was sworn in, MacNelly announced he was taking a leave of absence to concentrate on his daily comic strip, Shoe, launched in 1978. Within six years, two more double dippers would be added to the contemporary cartooning scene: Doug Marlette, then of the *Charlotte Observer* and creator of Kudzu, and Mike Peters, of the *Dayton Daily News* and creator of Mother Goose and Grimm.

It was no surprise why comic strips enjoyed such renewed popularity. Doonesbury

Jerry Robinson, Cartoonists & Writers Syndicate, 1978. *In 1979 Carter was applauded for his success at negotiating a peace agreement between Israel's Manahem Begin and Egypt's Anwar Sadat. His ratings plummeted with the takeover of the American Embassy in Iran. The day that he left office fourteen months later, the U.S. hostages held in the Embassy were freed.*

Doug Marlette, *Charlotte Observer*, 1980.

Jim Borgman, *Cincinnati Enquirer*, November 14, 1979.

Jim Borgman, *Cincinnati Enquirer*, January 20, 1981.

Jeff MacNelly, *Chicago Tribune*, October 2, 1980.

had taken firm hold on America. Its creator, Garry Trudeau, seemed particularly sage in presenting the basic mistrust of the governed toward their government. Trudeau had won the Pulitzer Prize in 1975—the first prize for editorial cartooning ever awarded to a comic strip. His strip was consistently political and controversial. Its fictional characters, like Zonker Harris and Joanie Caucus, regularly referenced current news events and known personalities. Carried in more than 400 newspapers with a readership of more than sixty million, "Doonesbury" often made news itself. "There are only three major vehicles to keep us informed as to what is going on in Washington," President Ford said in 1976, "the electronic media, the print media and Doonesbury and not necessarily in that order."

Presidents are a cartoonist's bread and butter. Since each new chief executive becomes the symbol for his term in office, cartoonists sweat to arrive at the essence of the man they will draw repeatedly. For *Newsday* cartoonist Doug Marlette, that caricature was key: "Cartoonists are after that certain quality that comes through despite everything that makeup artists, speech writers, spin doctors and press secretaries do to hide it.... We want his soul." As they did with Teddy Roosevelt, cartoonists doted on the affable and popular President Reagan, not necessarily because they liked his politics, but because he made their job easier.

Reagan told history as Hollywood might reconfigure it, referring to the Soviet Union as the Evil Empire, a proposed space-based defense system as Star Wars, and rebel soldiers in Nicaragua as freedom fighters. Cartoonists at-

Don Wright, *Miami News*, March 30, 1982.

Jeff MacNelly, *Chicago Tribune*, 1988.

David Levine, *New York Review of Books*, 1981.

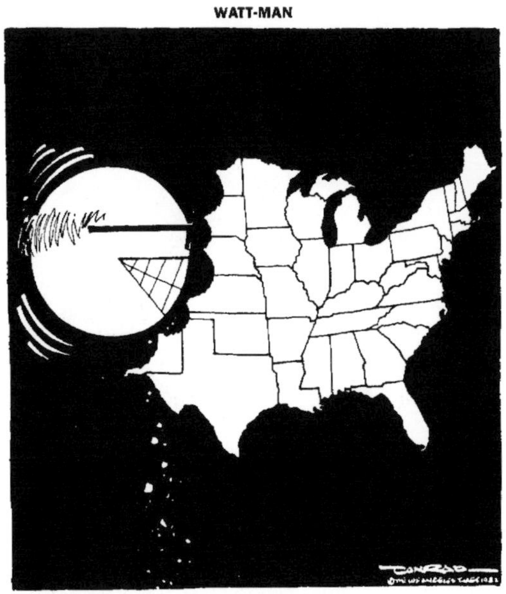

LEFT: Paul Conrad, *Los Angeles Times*, March 26, 1982. RIGHT: Doug Marlette, *Charlotte Observer*, July 16, 1981. *Secretary of Interior James Watt's aggressive plans to radically alter long-standing environmental policies gave cartoonists a new bad guy. Conrad's "Watt-Man" played off the then-popular video game, Pac-man. Marlette chose Bambi to symbolize the destructive potential of Watt's policies. Bambi continues to be used as a symbol, but Pac-man, used by many cartoonists during the game's span of popularity, had a short life.*

tacked Reagan's environmental policies, zeroing in on Secretary of the Interior James Watt's plans for privatizing Alaska's oil and gas and clear-cutting national forests. None presented these issues better than Don Wright, whose style and searing point of view had long provided inspiration to younger cartoonists. Many called him "the cartoonist's cartoonist."

Wright joined the *Miami News* in 1952, right out of high school. He would hold the position of copyboy, photographer, and graphics editor before becoming the paper's editorial cartoonist in 1963. For Wright there has never been any distinction between a journalist and an editorial cartoonist. He took an active part in the editorial decisions of his paper, not only sitting in on editorial meetings, but in determining the day-to-day direction of the paper.

Like Wright, Tony Auth sat in on his paper's editorial meetings. When he interviewed for the job at the *Philadelphia Inquirer* in 1971, he sat in on the daily editorial meetings and has continued to attend the morning conferences ever since. "I enjoy hearing the divergent points of view," Auth said. "I don't always agree with them, but it makes me think—how do I counteract that [point of view]?" His cartoons,

Don Wright, *Miami News*, circa 1970s.

LEFT: Bill Day, *Detroit Free Press*, April 6, 1986. RIGHT: Jim Borgman, *Cincinnati Enquirer*, April 29, 1985. *"We Are the World" became a popular song in 1985. Jim Borgman played off his audience's familiarity with the tune, changing the lyrics to fit the news that President Reagan had been secretly sending caches of arms to Nicaragua.*

which won him a Pulitzer Prize in 1976, are not discussed or reviewed at the meeting. His work during the Reagan years was delightful and deceptively simple.

As Reagan's administration drew to a close, the Iran-Contra affair, in which weapons sold to Iran had provided a secret cache of money to support the rebel fighters called Contras in Nicaragua, was revealed. Oliver North testified before a congressional committee investigating the matter in 1987, admitting to lying to Congress and shredding documents. Reactions to North were mixed: many saw him as a hero, others as the ghost of Richard Nixon.

Jim Borgman walked right into a cartooning job after college in 1976 at his hometown paper, the *Cincinnati Enquirer.* The first few years at the drawing board were his baptism by fire. He quickly found that while he had the drawing skills necessary for the position, his politics and his opinions still needed honing. "I think our profession has swung in a crazy way toward the assumption that from the beginning we're supposed to know what we stand for and how to express it best," Borgman said. "I think that I have probably spent more dark hours wondering about where I stand on issues than I have wondering how to draw them." The Midwesterner's calling card would become his ability to put national news within the context of his readers' day-to-day routine. His humor was derived

through juxtaposition. His cartoons often depicted Mr. and Mrs. America as they sat in their living room reacting to the news on their television set or as they read the morning paper at the breakfast table.

Just as Joseph Keppler had stripped away the hypocrisy he saw at all levels of society in 1884, a hundred years later Borgman and his contemporaries found that they had as much to say about societal ills as about political events. This renewed trend toward doing more cartoons on social issues reflected growing concerns about the environment, crime, and education. Wayne Stayskal, the cartoonist for the *Tampa Tribune,* found his most effective work came when he used humor to chip away at the confusion and contradictions life in the United States presented. Stayskal was not a newcomer to cartooning—he had been schooled by Chicago's Vaughn Shoemaker during the 1960s—but his style had grown looser as his message grew more distinct over the years. His

LEFT: Tom Toles, *Buffalo News*, July 7, 1987. RIGHT: Paul Szep, *Boston Globe*, July 1987. ***The Senate and House held investigations in 1987 to determine who was responsible for the Iran-Contra cover-up. When Oliver North testified, he invoked the Fifth Amendment's protection. Many felt the handsome colonel was hiding behind his chest of medals. During the year-long hearings, each witness in turn pointed the finger at his superior. North charged that CIA Director William Casey, who had died before the investigation started, had masterminded the arms-for-hostages plan.***

Jim Borgman, *Cincinnati Enquirer*, June 10, 1990.

was a call for America to reexamine its moral fabric, presented with a refreshing and droll approach, dramatically different from what his apprenticeship might suggest. Stayskal joined MacNelly as one of the few conservative cartoonists with a permanent position on a paper.

Many cartoonists bringing new approaches to political cartoons were to emerge during the 1980s. Invited by Washington Post editor Meg Greenfield to incorporate the strip he had created for the *Village Voice* into a Washington-focused cartoon, Mark Stamaty checked into the Washington Hilton and hung out at the Post newsroom to get a feeling for his new turf and its cast of characters. "Washingtoon," which ran each Monday on the Post's op-ed page, soon had an avid following. Tom Toles started working for his hometown paper, the *Buffalo News*, as an editorial cartoonist in 1982. Toles thought of himself as an illustrator, not a cartoonist, and before he agreed to take on the cartoonist's yoke, he researched the history of the craft and its practitioners, looking for a personal approach with which he could feel comfortable. Jeff Danziger served in Vietnam and taught school for ten years before he joined the cartooning ranks. He approached his panel at the *Christian*

ABOVE:
Michael Ramirez,
***The Memphis Commercial Appeal*,**
April 20, 1994.

BELOW:
Wayne Stayskal,
***Tampa Tribune*,**
October 29, 1993.

LEFT: Jim Borgman, *Cincinnati Enquirer*, November 17, 1988. ***George H.W. Bush chose Dan Quayle as his running mate. Quayle was perceived as a lightweight, a characterization he never overcame.***

RIGHT: Kevin Kallaugher, *Baltimore Sun*, August 1, 1991. ***Bush and USSR President Gorbachev came head to head on the issue of reducing nuclear warheads.***

Science Monitor with daring—often stark—compositions. The *Monitor* had an international readership, and Danziger commented on world affairs with more frequency than many of his colleagues.

Where once cartoons on foreign affairs were limited to times of war or catastrophe, now, thanks to the Cable News Network (CNN), readers talked about news events unfolding around the globe. With their scope of inquiry thus widened, cartoonists commented regularly on the dramatic changes in the Soviet Union, Eastern Europe, Africa, and the Middle East. During the Bush administration, Desert Storm became a television war with enemy and ally, military strategist and television viewer alike relying on the same television coverage for their news.

Kevin "Kal" Kallaugher had been at the *Baltimore Sun* two years when Desert Storm began in 1991. "When the American government and military called on all journalists to be patriots, I reveled in the opportunity to challenge some of those thoughts," Kallaugher said. "The news was breaking by the hour. So many people were well informed over what the issues were you didn't have to do explana-

"GOOD LORD! THE SOVIET UNION HAS VANISHED!"

LEFT: Etta Hulme, *Fort Worth Star-Telegram*, February 19, 1991.

BELOW: Mike Peters, *Dayton Daily News*, February 2, 1990.

During the George H. W. Bush Administration, the world saw the collapse of the Soviet Union and the rise of a new era under the leadership of Mikhail Gorbachev. American business poured into Russia to exploit the country's new capitalist direction. A McDonalds restaurant opened in the heart of Moscow.

tory cartoons setting up the issues. You could go to another level. It was one of those times when being a journalist was fun." Unlike many of his colleagues who used a minimalist cartoon style, Kallaugher's use of detailed crosshatching was reminiscent of an era gone by, when weekly—not daily—deadlines were the norm, but his sense of composition was bold and decidedly contemporary.

TRY IT COMRADE... IT'S CALLED A "HAPPY MEAL."

ABOVE: Tony Auth, *Philadelphia Inquirer*, February 21, 1991.

LEFT: Kevin Kallaugher, *Baltimore Sun*, December 2, 1990.
In 1990, Iraq's president Saddam Hussein moved to enlarge his sphere of influence in the Middle East by invading his oil-rich neighbor,Kuwait. Led by the United States, a multi-national force poured into the region and in January 1991 launched a decisive air and ground assault in which Iraqi forces were soundly defeated.
In 2003, in the aftermath of 9/11, the U.S. spearheaded a new assault called Operation Iraqi Freedom. Bagdad fell in 21 days, but Saddam Hussein escaped and evaded searchers for nine months. Ironically, he was eventually found hiding in an underground cellar much like the one Auth had drawn 12 years earlier.

Jeff Danziger, *Christian Science Monitor*, 1991.

So what if I have an abortion, Adam, who'll ever know?

RIGHT: Wayne Stayskal, *Chicago Tribune*, 1979.

BELOW: Signe Wilkinson, *Philadelphia Daily News*, 1992.

Doug Marlette, *Charlotte Observer*, 1981.

Mike Peters, *Dayton Daily News*, June 29, 1982.

Mike Peters, *Dayton Daily News*, October 17, 1991.

During the George H.W. Bush Administration, feminist perspectives that had surged during the debates on the Equal Rights Amendment in the 1970s and 1980s became a dominant theme in cartoons once again. The nomination of Clarence Thomas to the Supreme Court in 1991 brought the question of sexual harassment in the workplace to center stage. As Congress turned a sympathetic ear to the sworn statements of Thomas supporters, Signe Wilkinson, one of a handful of women cartoonists with permanent positions on newspapers, offered a strong counterpoint to the hearing-room testimony. In 1994 she became the first woman cartoonist to win a Pulitzer Prize. Although Wilkinson was not alone in her reactions to Thomas's confirmation, she often felt that she must be the standard-bearer for women's issues. "There are fewer black and women editorial cartoonists than there are blacks or women in the Senate," she said. "Aspiring satirists of color or breasts wisely skip this dying medium and go directly to film or the Fox channel, but it leaves a rather pale, breast-challenged contingent at the drawing board." In the early 1900s, as women sought the right to vote, the male-dominated cartooning profession made fun of the suffragettes' demands. Today's cartoonists are advocates for equal pay and freedom from sexual harassment, although issues of abortion continue to produce cartoons that split between "prochoice" and "prolife."

The Clarence Thomas nomination also brought "Doonesbury" back into the headlines. Throughout the Bush administration, Trudeau increasingly used his strip to reveal events that were largely ignored by the media. His feisty maven of Capitol Hill, Rep. Lacey Davenport, brought to the readers' attention the question of why testimony potentially damaging to Thomas was slipped into the record rather than presented in person. Davenport read this testimony to the "Doonesbury" audience. In a second incident, after President Bush declared a hotel room in Texas (not his residences in Washington, D.C., or Maine) as his primary residence in order to avoid higher state taxes, Trudeau invited readers to write the Texas state comptrol-

Garry Trudeau, *Doonesbury*, Universal Press Syndicate, February 1992.

ler and declare their "intention to live in Texas ...and save big—just like the President." More than 30,000 inquiries were received.

"Doonesbury" had become a vehicle for printing in the comic pages what journalists had omitted from the news pages. Referring to the Thomas testimony, Bill Kovach, curator of the Nieman fellowship program for journalists at Harvard and former editor of the *Atlanta Constitution*, said, "It raises the question as to why Garry Trudeau [had to do it] as opposed to the news department. Trudeau was raising a legitimate issue." Writing about the incident and Garry Trudeau's impact, *Charlotte Observer* editor Richard Oppel concluded, "He's a serious journalist who happens to use the medium of cartoons."

The race for the White House in 1992 was little different than any other since William Jennings Bryan had turned presidential campaigning into a full-time job in 1896. Cartoonists, a predominantly liberal group, rallied around the camp of Bill Clinton, the southern governor who cast himself in a reflection of John F. Kennedy in his race against incumbent George Bush. The campaign was enlivened by the appearance, disappearance, and reappearance of third-party candidate Ross Perot, whose popularity underlined the public's discontent with the major parties.

The election brought the Democrats back into the White House for the first time in twelve years. Any hopes that Clinton would bring a new Camelot to Washington, however, quickly vanished. Before his first month in office was completed, the President, aided and abetted by an ambitious but naive staff, was in trouble. Controversy piled on innuendo—a proposal to allow gays in the military; ongoing reports of Clinton's extramarital affairs; and the announcement that his health care team would be headed by his wife, Hillary Rodham Clinton. Within a year the health care proposal was shelved, and Clinton labeled as indecisive.

Jeff MacNelly, *Chicago Tribune*, October 14, 1992.

Tom Toles, *Buffalo News*, August 30, 1992.

Herbert Block, *Washington Post*, November 6, 1992.

RIGHT: Don Wright, *Palm Beach Post*, Fall 1993.

BELOW: Pat Oliphant, Universal Press Syndicate, 1995.

Midterm congressional elections in 1994 brought in the first Republican Congress since 1954 and a new House majority leader, Newt Gingrich. Television talk shows and cartoonists loved Newt. He was brisk, charged with a mission, and spoke his mind. As banner-carrier for the traditional Republican ideals of less government, welfare, and taxes, Gingrich challenged Clinton's agenda at every opportunity. Bitter partisan debates arose between the two parties over a balanced budget, and a failure to reach a compromise forced two controversial shutdowns of the government.

Far more Americans tuned in to the daily coverage of the O.J. Simpson trial in 1995 than had watched C-SPAN's coverage of the budget debate. The case centered on whether the black celebrity had killed his white wife and her companion, but a far greater issue lurked behind every clash between the prosecution and defense—the chasm between black and white America. It has remained one of the biggest problems facing the country, and one that cartoonists are only beginning to tackle head-on.

Perhaps more than any other issue, the nation's racial division has been the hardest for cartoonists to confront. They and their editors had sidestepped the challenge in the 1960s and 1970s when they failed to include the caricatures and messages of Martin Luther King Jr. and other African American leaders, opting for predictable, almost saccharine, metaphors on poverty. Although local and state politicians—especially black mayors in the nation's larger cities—had come between the cartoonists' cross hairs, it was not until Jesse Jackson became a candidate for the presidential nomination in 1984 that cartoonists began to use barbed caricatures of prominent blacks on a regular basis. Today Clarence Thomas, Colin Powell, and other notable black Americans are treated with the same irreverence as notable white Americans.

As each minority group demanded a reconfiguration of its image and appellation in the mainstream press in the 1990s, "political correctness" had become more than a trend for cartoonists; it had become a bad joke. "American society is increasingly preoccupied with offending and being offended," said *Boston Globe* cartoonist Dan Wasserman. "Rather than reply to an argument or cartoon with which they disagree by saying 'I disagree,' more and more people are saying 'I'm offended.' They insist that their subjective state is someone

ABOVE: Jack Ohman, *The Oregonian*, October 4, 1995.

BELOW: Steve Benson, *Arizona Republic*, November 10, 1995.

Signe Wilkinson, *Nation*, January 17, 1994.

else's objective problem and they demand redress." Satire will always offend someone, and for cartoonists to bring commentary on racial diversity back into their rectangular boxes might indicate that these issues can now be discussed.

In 1993, a year after he retired from daily cartooning, *Los Angeles Times* cartoonist Paul Conrad criticized a gathering of the country's best cartoonists for opting for gags, a term used to describe funny cartoons that have no discernible point of view. Gags had been a familiar cop-out in the face of controversy throughout the history of cartooning, but the trend, many feared, was now taking over the industry. "Illustrating the news is not what we're about," Conrad said. "Our job is to be subjective—to have an opinion." Conrad's speech was a wake-up call to a new generation of cartoonists.

How would they respond?

Tom Toles, of the *Buffalo News,* argued that political cartoons can do more than contribute anecdotally to the political debate, that "under the right circumstances they can help mold it. I realized that if you get good enough and consistent enough and read widely enough, you can actually make a difference." In 2001 he would be chosen to take Herb Block's chair at the *Washington Post.*

Toles' colleague at the Post, columnist Kathleen Parker, also offered her thoughts on cartoons' impact: "... humor is mostly a pleasant test of our allegiance to founding principles. Think of it this way: The degree to which one can tolerate ribbing about one's most deeply held convictions if the degree to which a society can remain free. We honor that notion through our laws and our sense of humor."

CARTOONING AT A CROSSROADS: 1997 - 2010

Gordon Campbell, *www.cagle.com*, June 12, 2008.

MARCH 6, 2008. GORDON CAMPBELL didn't expect the pink slip. He had survived California's *Inland Valley Daily Bulletin's* other rounds of layoffs and his daily cartoons were now being carried by fifty additional papers nationwide in the MediaNews chain. With the 2008 presidential contest off to a rollicking start in Iowa and New Hampshire, life was good for Campbell—or so it seemed: "I'll be damned if my cartoons weren't getting better and better as the conflict raged. But… there was an ominous soundtrack playing in the background…. The guillotine was wheeling into the newsroom!"

Campbell's job was one of the many local and national cartoonist positions lost to downward spiraling readership and revenues for newspapers throughout the United States. Since 2005 over thirty cartoonists have lost their jobs. Some took voluntary buyouts; others were unceremoniously laid off. It may have been the Tribune Company that started the death march for print cartoonists when, in November 2005, it announced that the services of two of the medium's most respected practitioners, the *Los Angeles Times'* Michael Ramirez and Kevin "KAL" Kallaugher of the *Baltimore Sun*, were no longer needed. The *Chicago Tribune*, the company's flagship paper, had left vacant the staff cartoonist position for nine years after the death of Jeff MacNelly in 2000. In the future, most papers would pick up cartoons on the cheap from syndicates rather than hire their own artists. Collum Rogers, the American Association of Editorial Cartoonists' unofficial historian, reports that full-time staff cartoonist jobs on newspapers or periodicals nationwide have been cut in half over the past twenty years. Around seventy-five full time positions remain. Ted Rall, the popular syndicated cartoonist, says cartoonists are "the canary in the coal mine" for the newspaper industry.

Yet it's impossible to kill the desire to take aim at politicians and public events in picture. Cartoonists will continue to probe the highs and lows of the national psyche. Here are some of their memorable contributions from 1997 to 2010.

William Jefferson Clinton's first four years in office were a love-in for cartoonists. They couldn't help themselves. David Horsey of the *Seattle Post-Intelligencer* had accompanied Clinton when he campaigned in New Hampshire in 1992. As the 1996 election swung into gear, with allegations of Clinton's extramarital affairs continuing to make headlines, Horsey decided he needed to create a new symbol for "The American People" and came up with a bosomy brunette wearing a tight T-shirt with "America" emblazoned on it. She perfectly caricatured the country's love/hate relationship with its president. Then came 1998 and Monica Lewinsky. Horsey did a double take. His "America" was her spitting image. The *Seattle Post-Intelligencer* cartoonist received his first Pulitzer Prize for what he calls "the year of Monica."

Nick Anderson, December 12, 2005.

Cartoonists across the country protested the Tribune Company's firing of two respected colleagues, Michael Ramirez and Kevin Kallaugher. Anderson's cartoon spotlighted the Chicago Tribune's landmark tower that had housed the studios of the paper's long string of Pulitzer Prize winning cartoonists since it was built in 1925 (See page 77).

ABOVE:
Horsey self-caricature.

ABOVE RIGHT: David Horsey, *Seattle Post-Intelligencer*, May 6, 1996.

BELOW: David Horsey, *Seattle Post-Intelligencer*, July 7, 1999.

The Lewinsky affair made cartoonists—along with the rest of America—uncomfortable. Herb Block, who had been surfing politics at the *Washington Post* since 1946, remarked to a conference of cartoonists and editors, "Most of us feel we'd rather this thing never happened ... but even when President Clinton appeared on television to say he wanted forgiveness, he wagged his finger and told us just as sincerely how he never had relations with this woman." As cartoonists struggled to keep up with daily revelations on what was happening in the Oval Office, Pat Oliphant noted, "In Clinton's case, reality is ahead of satire. We have to play catch up every day." Clinton was impeached in 1998, becoming only the second sitting president in U.S. history to receive such a dubious honor. (The first was Andrew Johnson in 1868.) Tried in the Senate, Clinton was acquitted of all charges.

Horsey retired his sexy "America" when the Bush Administration came to power. "It quickly became a whole different scenario."

Kevin Kallaugher, *The Economist*, November 11, 2000.

November 7, 2000 provided a cliff-hanger of a presidential election. The choice, between Vice President Albert Gore and Texas Governor George W. Bush, came down to Florida's 1700 contested votes. The problem was "hanging chads," those little dots that get punched out from a paper ballot. If the "chad" wasn't fully separated from the ballot, it was deemed "hanging." Some election officials interpreted an unseparated chad as an undecided vote; others did not. The Florida Supreme Court decreed that a county-by-county recount was in order, but the U.S. Supreme Court stepped in and overturned the recount, thereby giving Bush the state—and the election. Although Gore won the popular count by over 500,000 ballots, the deciding electoral vote tally was Bush 271, Gore 266.

ABOVE LEFT: Mike Ritter,
Tribune Newspapers, Phoenix Arizona, November, 2002.

ABOVE RIGHT: Jeff Danziger, New York Times Syndicate, December 13, 2000.

BELOW RIGHT: Ann Telnaes, December 13, 2000.

Ann Telnaes on U.S. Supreme Court decision: "I had the five justices who voted to stop the recount open their robes and show their true political colors."

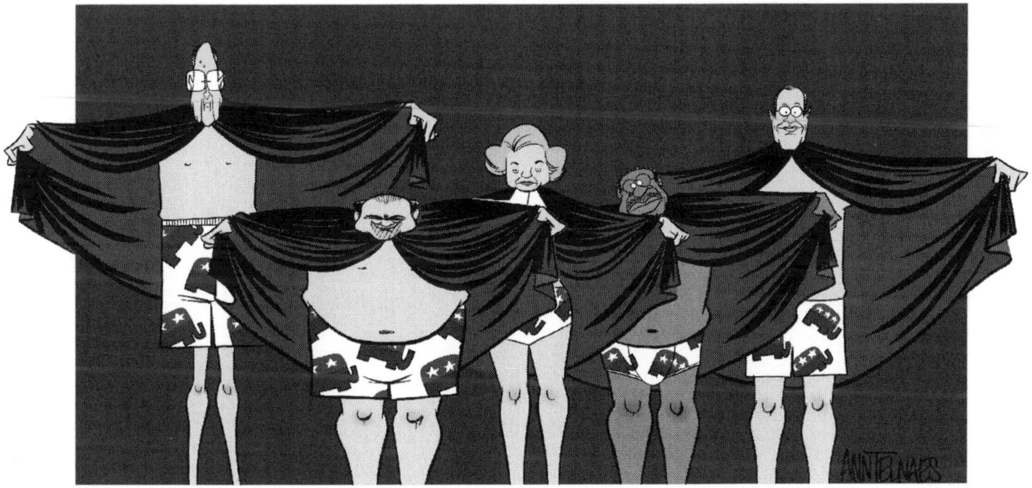

12/13/00

LEFT: Mike Luckovich. *Atlanta Journal-Constitution*, September 12, 2001. *Neither Luckovich nor his editor liked this cartoon, but the paper's readers did. The* Atlanta Journal-Constitution *printed full-color posters of the cartoon, sold them and raised $250,000 for the 9/11 Fund.* RIGHT: Dana Summers, *Orlando Sentinel*, September 13, 2001.

President Bush had been in office only eight months when terrorists struck the United States on September 11, 2001. Around the country—and the world—people stared at their televisions in disbelief as the two 110-story towers of New York's World Trade Center crumbled after being hit by two planes commandeered by terrorists. A third plane struck the Pentagon outside Washington, D.C. A fourth plane crashed in the Pennsylvania countryside. Nearly 3000 died, including 411 firemen, police, and paramedic workers. Thousands more were wounded.

Over the next two weeks, as patriotism soared, editorial cartoonists returned to the tried-and-true symbols of Uncle Sam and Lady Liberty to express the nation's grief. But few cartoons could compete with the devastating televised images of the terrorists' attacks and their aftermath that replayed constantly. *Atlanta Journal-Constitution* cartoonist Mike Luckovich explained, "After September 11th, you just couldn't use humor. The tragedy was so enormous, you couldn't be funny. It's almost like you have to come up with cartoons using a different part of your brain. I was just trying to come up with

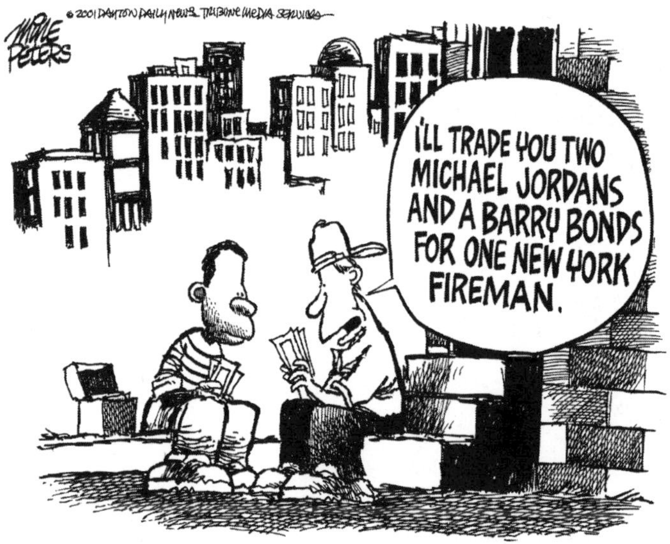

LEFT: Mike Ritter, *Tribune Newspapers*, Phoenix, Arizona, September 12, 2001. RIGHT: Mike Peters, *Dayton Daily News*, September 12, 2001.
Rescue workers at the World Trade Center quickly became the new heroes of the day.

images that expressed the emotions that I was feeling and tried to focus in on different aspects of the tragedy that I thought were important."

Christopher Lamb, a professor at the College of Charleston and a respected cartoon analyst, noted that following 9/11 cartoonists gave the Bush Administration the benefit of the doubt: Garry Trudeau canceled a series of *Doonesbury* strips critical of the president. Even Pat Oliphant was sympathetic, saying cartoonists had to support the administration—at least for the time being. During World War I, the Bureau of Cartoons recruited cartoonists to support the war effort, now many signed up voluntarily. (See page 82.)

When cartoonists get together, they still disagree over what the proper response to the 9/11 tragedy should have been. Ann Telnaes argues, "As a whole, editorial cartoonists were slow to break free of flag-waving images, what I call the red/white/blue cartoons. Jingoism colored many cartoons and self-censorship, whether voluntary or a reaction to editorial pressure, was very evident in the work of cartoonists after 9/11." Professor Lamb agrees: "Nothing is more patriotic than social criticism. The First Amendment doesn't exist so we can praise public officials; it exists so we can criticize them."

Clay Bennett, *Christian Science Monitor*, October 29, 2001.

Clay Bennett was working for the *Christian Science Monitor* when the Office of Homeland Security and the USA Patriot Act were established in October 2001. He remembers his thoughts: "I knew what was coming. This country has a long history of dissembling our liberties during times of strife—this goes back to 1798 with the original Alien and Sedition Act and the Espionage Act of 1917." As his response to the Patriot Act, Bennett drew a suburban couple looking on helplessly as the sides of their home are pulled off and used to build a security fence—to suggest the balance the government needed to strike between national security and personal civil liberties.

Bennett focuses on issues not caricatures: "I've never had confidence in my ability to capture someone's likeness so I tend to draw more about issues than personalities. I think in the long run it's a better strategy because presidents change, politicians change, but the issues stay the same."

Clay Bennett, *Christian Science Monitor*, May 2, 2001.

Bennett self-caricature.

While Clay Bennett took a more liberal perspective, one of contemporary cartooning's few conservative voices, Michael Ramirez, penned the flip side of the national security versus civil rights debate. He felt the country had no choice but to be vigilant.

Michael Ramirez, *Los Angeles Times*, October 4, 2001.

John Deering, *Arkasas Democrat-Gazette*, Little Rock, September 20, 2001.

Mike Luckovich, *Atlanta Journal-Constitution*, October, 2002.

Jim Borgman, *Cincinnati Inquirer*, October, 2002.

Ed Gamble, *Florida Times-Union*, Jacksonville, August 11, 2002.

Michael Ramirez, *Los Angeles Times*, October 2002.

After 9/11 everything changed. American response to the tragedy was swift. On October 7, 2001 U.S. military and coalition forces launched "Operation Enduring Freedom" to drive Osama Bin Laden and Al-Qaeda out of Afghanistan. Terrorists, it seemed, were everywhere, even on U.S. shores and Americans felt vulnerable. But when Tom Ridge, the Office of Homeland Security chief, unveiled a "terror alert code" in early 2002, the futility of trying to contain such an elusive enemy with a color code made more than just cartoonists wince.

President Bush declared a "war on terrorism." On October 7, 2001, U.S. planes bombed Afghanistan.

ABOVE: David Horsey, *Seattle Post-Intelligencer*, June 28, 2003. *Horsey keeps a framed quote from President John F. Kennedy on his desk: "There are three things that are real: God, human folly and laughter. The first two are beyond comprehension, so we must do what we can with the third."*

RIGHT: Jeff Stahler, *USA Today*, August 28, 2002. *After 9/11, it seemed clear to many that it was Vice President Cheney—not George W. Bush—who was giving the orders.*

It soon became clear that the Administration saw Afghanistan as only a stepping-stone to Saddam Hussein. Weapons of mass destruction (WMD) were the reason offered to take the war into Iraq. Congress put up scant resistance to the White House plan, voting to support an invasion, although it was later shown that Iraq had no weapons of mass destruction. U.S. forces entered Baghdad on April 5th. Four days later, Hussein's statue was toppled but he and his sons escaped. The celebration that accompanied Saddam's overthrow quickly turned to pillaging. Museums, banks, hotels,and libraries were ransacked. Sectarian fighting followed.

Frank Cammuso, *Post-Standard*, Syracuse, NY, May 4, 2003.

Tony Auth, *Philadelphia Inquirer*, November 13, 2003.

On May 1, 2003, only fifty days after the invasion of Iraq, President Bush, dressed in an Air Force flight suit, emerged from the jet he had copiloted on to the deck of the aircraft carrier U.S.S. Abraham Lincoln. With a banner reading "Mission Accomplished" stretched behind him, and thousands of cheering Navy personnel looking on, the president announced: "My fellow Americans, major combat operations in Iraq have ended… And now our coalition is engaged in securing and reconstructing that country." It was a stage set and a speech that would come to haunt him.

In November 2006 Iraq's Health Minister estimated between 100,000 and 150,000 Iraqis had been killed since the war began in March 2003. Many of these deaths were attributed to suicide bombers, many recruited by the Taliban, who gave up their lives for their cause. For their children's sacrifice, parents of these "martyrs" reportedly received substantial monetary rewards.

ABOVE LEFT: Chris Britt, *The State Journal-Register*, Springfield, Il., April 8, 2002.

ABOVE RIGHT: Walt Handelsman, *Newsday*, Melville, NY, November 28, 2006.

OPPOSITE LEFT: Ann Telnaes, December 31, 2006. *After the invasion of Baghdad, Saddam Hussein escaped and hid from American forces for over nine months. He became the nemesis of George Bush and the American people. Discovered hiding in the basement of a farmhouse, he was tried for war crimes, found guilty and executed December 30, 2006.*

OPPOSITE RIGHT: Ann Telnaes, May 7, 2003. *Americans began to question the huge profits private contractors were reaping for supplying U.S. forces in Iraq. One such company was Halliburton. Prior to becoming vice president, Richard Cheney was its CEO.*

Ann Telnaes became one of President Bush's most persistent critics. Her razor-sharp focus on the Oval Office's failures may have been responsible for her meteoric rise in editorial cartooning. In 2001 she became the first freelancer to win the Pulitzer Prize. Two years later, the Library of Congress honored her with a one-person show, an honor given to only three other living cartoonists: Herb Block, Pat Oliphant, and Jules Feiffer.

In 1989, Telnaes was working as a designer for Disney's Imagineering division when she drew her first political cartoon after listening to reports of the brutal treatment meted out to student demonstrators in China's Tiananmen Square. When Telnaes moved to Washington, D.C. in 1993, she decided to make political cartooning her full-time job: "Before that I was just drawing. That's fine. But for me, what really clicks is being able to take art and your thoughts and make a statement." Yet it is her elegant brush style—the result of many years of training in design and animation at the California Institute of the Arts—that has made Telnaes' work so distinctive.

Telnaes self-caricature.

RJ Matson, *The New York Observer*, July 28 2004.

The 2004 election between President Bush and the Democratic candidate, Senator John Kerry, would be a referendum on the war in Iraq. In the midst of an already ugly campaign, an organization calling itself "Swift Boat Veterans for Truth" alleged that Kerry, a decorated Vietnam hero, had lied about many of his wartime exploits. Kerry lost the election and "Swiftboating" became a term synonymous with smear campaign tactics.

Jeff Danziger, New York Times Service, June 25, 2005.

When recruiting efforts bogged down in 2005, the U.S. Army began offering monetary inducements to meet its goals. Danziger suggested recruiters use the same ploy as Al-Qaeda, which reportedly promised their suicide bombers that there would be seventy-two virgins awaiting them in heaven.

As each anniversary of the Iraq invasion passed, the hope of turning the country into a democracy remained elusive. Sectarian strife increased. The fighting among Sunnis and Shiites was now dubbed a civil war. In northern Iraq, the Kurds who sat on most of the oil wealth demanded autonomy. Massive improvised explosive devices (IEDs) planted along roadsides killed and maimed GIs; suicide bombers—both male and female—plowed headlong into markets and cafes killing Iraqi citizens. Countries that had initially provided military support began to withdraw their forces. U.S. soldiers were increasingly asked to carry most of the burden. Poor protective armor for both the soldiers and the vehicles plagued war efforts and army morale. GIs had served a single twelve-month tour during the Vietnam War. Now many soldiers would return to the battlefields of Iraq and Afghanistan three, four, even five times.

Advances in medical procedures coupled with the efficiency with which the wounded were whisked off the battlefield meant that many soldiers who might have died in Vietnam now lived. Twenty-four percent of the Americans injured in combat in Vietnam had died. In the wars in Iraq and Afghanistan, only about ten percent of those injured died, but many wounded soldiers would live out their lives with horrific injuries, including brain traumas and multiple limb amputations. Garry Trudeau documented the obstacles these soldiers confronted. He first began drawing his comic strip, *Doonesbury*, during the Vietnam War. Since then he has chronicled every war in which the United States has participated from the soldiers' perspective. But it came as a shock to his readers when in April 2004, B.D.,

Mike Keefe, *Denver Post*, March 8, 2007.

Garry Trudeau, *Doonesbury*, Universal Press Syndicate, August 24, 2004.

one of the strip's most enduring characters, was wounded in Iraq and lost a leg.

The cartoonist detailed every step of B.D.'s nine-month progression from triage center to VA hospital, from rehab to bouts with post-traumatic stress disorder. Trudeau has been visiting VA centers and talking to recovering vets since the first Iraq war. In 2006, *Army Times* correspondent Kelly Kennedy described Doonesbury's impact on soldiers in recovery. "He asked us to tell him our stories," said Staff Sgt. Daniel Metzdorf, who spent seven months at Walter Reed. "He'd visit and then you'd see some comment a soldier made show up in his comic strip. He's such a boost of morale for soldiers."

Tom Toles also followed the Iraq war's impact on America's warriors from his seat of power at the *Washington Post*. Toles, previously the cartoonist for the *Buffalo News*, was the *Post's* surprise choice to replace the venerated Herb Block after his death in 2001.

LEFT: Tom Toles, *Washington Post*, January 29, 2006. RIGHT: Tom Toles, *Washington Post*, October 19, 2004. *Even a year and a half into the war in Iraq, adequately armored military vehicles to protect soldiers against landmines were in short supply. Platoons began to solder scrap metal onto their vehicles. Mothers sent their sons "Care packages" containing body armor.*

Although Toles' deliberate child-like drawing style makes his cartoons appear less then confrontational, his commentary is searing. One 2006 cartoon on injured soldiers got a scathing response from the Pentagon brass: "Using the likeness of a service member who has lost his arms and legs in war as the central theme of a cartoon was beyond tasteless… As the joint chiefs, we rarely put our hand to one letter, but we cannot let this reprehensible cartoon go unanswered," wrote Peter Pace, General, U.S. Marine Corps, Chairman of the Joint Chiefs.

Other Post readers took issue with Pace's analysis: "I was a lowly sergeant in the Army, not a member of the Joint Chiefs, which is probably why I get the Tom Toles cartoon showing the Army as an amputee, with Defense Secretary Donald H. Rumsfeld making the kind of dismissive commentary on military challenges for which he is infamous. The cartoon was tasteless, but it wasn't pointless. This administration hides the coffins, the rehab wards and the force-

Toles self-caricature.

readiness statistics to protect itself from criticism of its mismanagement. It would like Americans to be oblivious to the financial and human cost of war." (Sergeant) Ronald M. Garrett, Morrisville, N.C.

Many called the harsh interrogation techniques used at U.S. prisons in Baghdad and Guantanamo "torture" as defined under the 1949 Geneva conventions. In 2004, photographs taken at Abu Ghraib showed prisoners being humiliated by their American prison guards. Detainees were forced to stand nude with hoods over their heads and electric wires attached to their bodies. Groups of naked men were stacked in compromising sexual positions while their guards took photographs. Following 9/11, cartoonists had a hard time competing with the stark photos the terrorist attacks produced. Abu Ghraib presented a similar situation. Cartoonists Kirk Anderson solved the problem by incorporating the Abu Ghraib photos directly into his drawings thereby adding his own commentary.

Kirk Anderson, *kirktoons.com*, May, 2004.

Ted Rall, *Boston Globe*, January 4, 2006. *Rall's caricature of George W. Bush was based on a photo he found of Chile's dictator Augusto Pinochet. "It was a state portrait. He's wearing a crazy sash, a giant hat and all these medals," Rall said. He felt the comparison fair. Rall's fans loved "Generalissimo."*

Ted Rall has emerged as the current "bad boy" among cartoonists, a moniker that has been proudly carried by Pat Oliphant, Bill Mauldin, and others. Rall is controversial and he relishes the role. The Right Wing News website named him 2003's "Most Annoying Liberal." Rall's drawings are distributed by Universal Press Syndicate. They are raw, outspoken, highly individualized, and very popular. He has become the ringleader for a gang of young, "alternative" cartoonists, including Mikhaela Reid, Stephanie McMillan, and Kevin Knight whose work thrives on the Internet and in a series of "Attitude" books that Rall edited. What unites these cartoonists, Rall wrote, is that they are "too alternative for the mainstream and too mainstream for the underground." Yet Rall hates the term, "alternative." He's done the math: "There are 185 alternative weeklies in the U.S. Each one runs an average of four cartoons. That's almost 800 cartoons!"

Rall self-caricature.

Mikhaela Reid, *Attack of the 50ft. Mikhaela*, 2007. *When the Abu Garaib story broke, Reid was appalled by what she characterized as the Bush Administration's duplicity: "They said we were going into Iraq because Saddam Hussein tortured people, then they turned around and did the same thing."*

Matt Wuerker, the cartoonist for *politico.com*, sees the transition to the Internet as inevitable. "There are so many market forces arrayed against having a staff cartoonist. Timid editorial page editors can skip having an over-opinionated character like a Paul Conrad down the hall who they have to manage, and just subscribe to syndicated cartoons. That way they can pick out the cartoons they know won't rankle readers or management, and perhaps most importantly, it's far cheaper than paying to have a cartoonist on staff." For Wuerker, the Internet has enormous appeal. "Websites have learned the value of cartoons. They understand that the Internet is a visual universe. They're putting cartoons on their homepages to draw in readers. *Politico* runs me off the homepage, the *Washington Post* is doing it, so is *Slate.com*. So maybe it's all coming full circle, back to where we were in the 19th century when cartoons were featured on the front page of many newspapers." Harry Katz, a former curator at the Library of Congress, agrees, "Technology is fundamentally changing the profession just as it has done since the 1400s. Technology works its changes, commerce works its changes and it's not the publishers who adapt, it's the cartoonists."

With news and political commentary moving to the Internet, newspapers now require staff cartoonists to maintain their own website (or contribute to the newspaper's site), monitor and respond to the correspondence it generates, while filing daily cartoons—both in color and black and white—on deadline. For the *Seattle Post-Intelligencer's* David Horsey, the changes have been fast and furious. In 2008, he explained how his workload had shifted: "I used to be much more active on our editorial board but now it's hard to find time to fit it in. The website has taken over." Less than a year later, in January 2009, the *Seattle Post-Intelligencer* abandoned its print edition and now exists solely as a web publication. Horsey was one of 20 staff members to hold on to his job taking a new moniker, editorial cartoonist for Hearst papers.

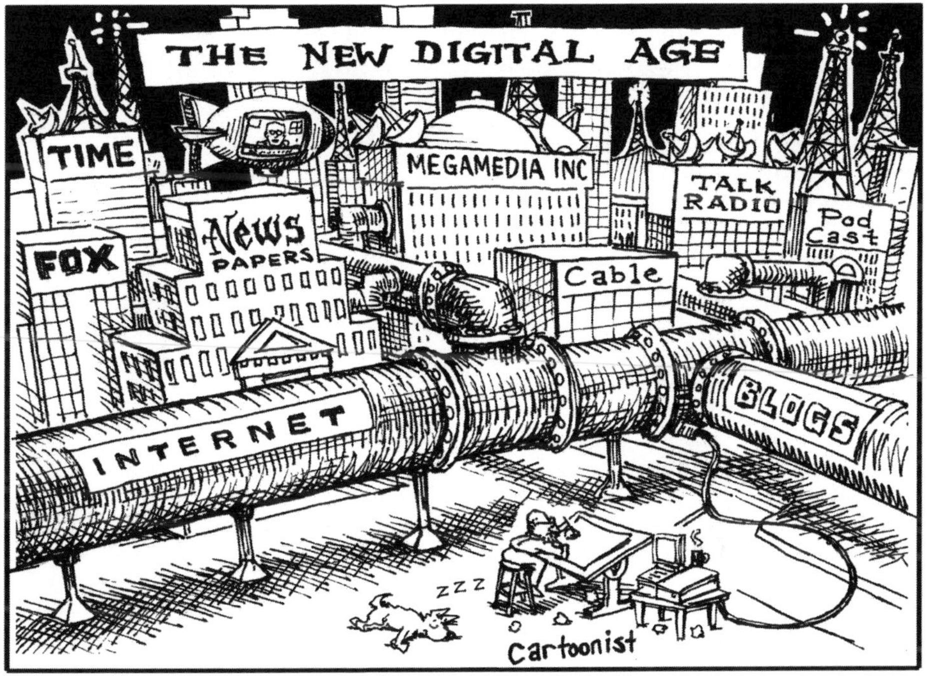

Matt Wuerker, *politico.com*, June 11, 2007.

Animated Editorial Cartoons from the 2008 Presidential Campaign.

Animation has rapidly become the new medium of choice for the under-50 generation of cartoonists. In 2001, Mark Fiore was the first cartoonist to leave penning a daily editorial cartoon to create weekly animations for *cbs.com*. Ann Telnaes followed in 2008, giving up daily cartooning to draw three animations a week for *washingtonpost.com*. "I needed to move on. I never made a living at editorial cartooning even after I won the Pulitzer," she said.

Mike Thompson at the *Detroit Free Press*, Nick Anderson at the *Houston Chronicle*, and Newsday's Walt Handelsman still stride both worlds. Handelsman did such a fine job juggling print and web animation that he won his second Pulitzer Prize in 2007 for a portfolio of ten print cartoons and ten animations. Yet doing an animation every two weeks was too much, he said. "Pulitzer schmulitzer. I couldn't keep up with that pace as long as I was a full-time editorial cartoonist." Handelsman has since cut back to one animation per month. Harry Katz, who now chairs the committee that gives out the annual Herblock Prize, contends that animation is not political cartooning. "We're struggling [in awarding] the Herblock Prize. Do we give a prize for animation? Do we make it one prize, like the Pulitzer has done? I think they are two different things." Times change. In 2010, the Herb Block Foundation shifted its policy and gave Matt Wuerker its award for a portfolio that included animation. That year also saw Mark Fiore become the first cartoonist to win a Pulitzer Prize for a portfolio consisting solely of animated editorial cartoons.

Television shows such as *Saturday Night Live*, Jon Stewart's *Daily Show*, and *The Colbert Report*, offer millions of Americans their news mixed with humor. Stephen Colbert compares the production of satire to "distilling a story to one shot of whiskey." Distilling the best of each day's political cartoons may be his secret source. A few cartoonists have begun doing their own "stand-ups." Steve Benson records weekly off-the-cuff reviews of his cartoons for the *Arizona Republic* website. Kevin Kallaugher has taken his show on the road. After the *Baltimore Sun* let him go in 2005, KAL turned adversity into opportunity and joined forces with the Imaging Research Center at the University of Maryland to create a three-dimensional "W" based on his George Bush caricatures. Five months later, they gave birth to a digital "W" who could walk and talk in real time. When the 2008 presidential race swung into gear, KAL hit the lecture circuit entertaining audiences with digital puppets of not only "W", but also Hillary Clinton, Barack Obama, and John McCain.

OPPOSITE PAGE, Clockwise from top left:

Walt Handelsman, Barack Obama, *newsday.com*, April 3, 2007.

Kevin Kallaugher, George W. Bush, *kaltoons.com*, Spring, 2006.

Mark Fiore, Hillary Clinton, *markfiore.com*, December, 19, 2007.

Ann Telnaes, Sarah Palin, *washingtonpost.com*, October 10, 2008.

Black cartoonists always have had to fight to have their cartoons syndicated beyond the black press. Aaron McGruder is a recent exception. His comic strip, *The Boondocks*, debuted in 1999 and explored themes never before seen in the comics. Through Huey (age 10) and Riley (age 8), two African American inner-city youths who have moved to the Chicago suburbs with their grandfather, McGruder presented his commentary on black America's racial adversities and other social pitfalls awaiting the boys in "the burbs." *The Boondocks* was an immediate syndicated success, paralleling Garry Trudeau's *Doonesbury* in both bite and popularity, but from a black perspective. In February 2006 McGruder announced a temporary hiatus from the comic pages. It later became permanent, when he, too, decided to abandon print for animation. In 2007 McGruder won a Peabody Award as the producer of a successful animated TV show based on *The Boondocks*' characters.

Aaron McGruder, *The Boondocks*, Universal Press Syndicate, November 22, 2001.

Lalo Alcaraz, the son of Mexican immigrants, takes his mission to be an advocate for Chicanos, Latinos, and immigrants very seriously. He deals primarily, but not exclusively, with political themes of concern to Latinos. In addition to a daily political cartoon, his comic strip, *La Cucaracha* (The Cockroach), debuted in newspapers nationwide in 2002. Its name demonstrates Alcaraz's ability to put forth issues that are important to him while maintaining a sense of humor. The term Cucaracha, he explains, symbolizes a people that cannot be exterminated. "The cucaracha will always be around and will survive you and me and all of our offspring." Is Alcaraz a crusader? He counters, "By definition, a Chicano is a politically conscious and self-aware Mexican American, so I'm just continuing a tradition of political advocacy and self-defense on behalf of my community."

La Cucaracha has a limited distribution, but its readers are very loyal. After one cartoon in September 2007, the *Houston Chronicle* announced it would no longer carry Alcaraz's strip in its print edition as it was "frequently inappropriate for a family newspaper." *La Cucaracha* was replaced with *Arctic Circle*, a strip featuring penguins. "You replaced a comic with biting commentary on the political and social scene with a strip about penguins?" one reader wrote.

ABOVE: Lalo Alcaraz, Universal Press Syndicate, 2000.

BELOW: Lalo Alcaraz, Border Muertes, *La Cucaracha*, 1998.

"Immigration is a hot-button issue in the country and central to my life," Alcaraz writes. "When times get tough, the tough bash immigrants." To depict the mounting hysteria against immigrants, Alcaraz took the southwest's "immigrant crossing" signs and repurposed them to create his own haunting images.

Ramirez self-caricature.

Michael Ramirez, like Lalo Alcaraz, grew up in southern California, the son of immigrants. Ramirez's dad is half Spanish, half Mexican; his mother is Japanese. The two cartoonists' politics, however, couldn't be wider apart. Ramirez, a staunch conservative, says his parents imparted to him the immigrant "can-do" spirit: "The coming to America and embracing all things that are American; and not taking these privileges—our rights—for granted."

In 1997, when Ramirez was chosen to replace Paul Conrad, one of cartooning's most liberal voices, the cartoon world, *Los Angeles Times* readers and Ramirez himself were surprised. "I was the only cartoonist that didn't apply for that job and was initially hesitant to take it. In fact, the first exchange I had with the editors was, 'I'm a capitalist, you guys are communists. This will never work.' I urged them to subscribe to my syndication to get a good idea of who I was." In the end, Ramirez took the job and over the next eight years punched home his conservative perspective with beautifully rendered cartoons every bit as strident as Paul Conrad's had been. "I was giving a speech one day and somebody asked me, 'Do you get death threats?' I said, 'I get death threats all the time, but the first death threat I got was when I told my parents I was going to become a journalist instead of a doctor.' All my brothers and sisters are doctors except for me." In 2005, Ramirez joined *Investor's Business Daily*.

Michael Ramirez, *Investor's Business Daily*, 2009.

LEFT: Bruce Plante, *The Chattanooga Times*, October 16, 2006.

BELOW: Steve Benson, *Arizona Republic*, Phoenix, April 18, 2006.

The immigrant issue has always been volatile, as is evidenced in Thomas Nast's and Joseph Keppler's depictions of the Irish, the Chinese and others during the late 1800s. (see pages 57, 61)

The current debate on how to balance the willingness of illegals to do jobs others shun is one for which no one—cartoonist or politician— has an answer. Steve Benson who lives in Arizona, a key border state with Mexico, does not shy away from continually putting the questions to his readers.

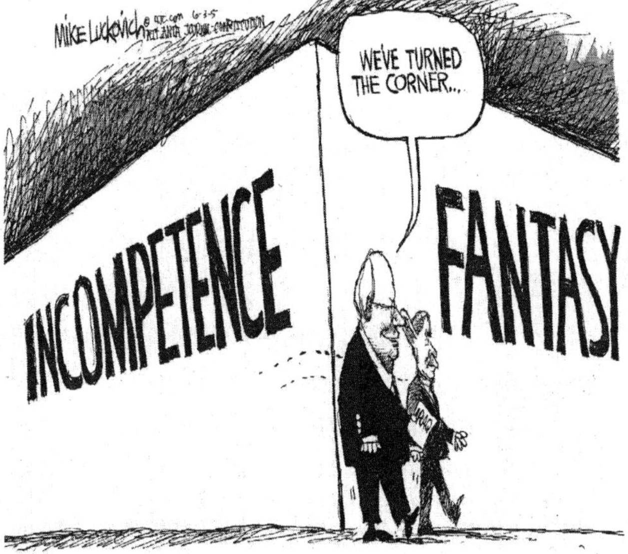

George W. Bush left the White House with the lowest approval ratings of any president in U.S. history. It was hard to find a cartoon of the president with a positive spin.

LEFT: Mike Luckovich, *Atlanta Journal-Constitution*, June 3, 2005.

BELOW: Paul Combs, *The Tampa Tribune*, April 24, 2006.

RIGHT: Nick Anderson, *Courier-Journal*, Louisville, September 12, 2005. ***When Hurricane Katrina devastated New Orleans, the federal government's response was slow and inadequate. Bush's popularity plummeted further.***

BELOW: Stuart Carlson, *Milwaukee Journal-Sentinel*, June 9, 2005. ***Congress' Committee on Oversight and Government Reform criticized the White House for engaging "in a systematic effort to manipulate climate change science and mislead policymakers and the public about the dangers of global warming."***

NEW MEDIA. ***The transition to the electronic age has reshaped every aspect of life in the 21st century. iPods and iTunes have replaced walkmans, records and DVDs. Text messaging, social networking and tweets are preferred to live conversation.***

ABOVE LEFT: Signe Wilkinson, *Philadelphia Daily News*, April 3, 2009. *President Obama presented Queen Elizabeth an iPod during his state visit in 2009.*

ABOVE RIGHT: Walt Handelsman, *Newsday*, Melville, NY, June 17, 2009. *As Iranian security forces hunted street protesters in Tehran by using Twitter location and time zone searches, around the world the under-thirties generation reprogrammed their Twitter accounts to match that of Iran, thereby foiling the security forces' efforts.*

BELOW RIGHT: Steve Kelley, *The Times-Picayune*, New Orleans, April 9, 2009.

Jim Borgman, *Cincinati Enquirer*, November 7, 1983. *Twenty-five years before such a historic race became a reality, Jim Borgman predicted that a white woman and a black man eventually would be presidential contenders.*

ABOVE RIGHT: Sandy Huffaker, *cagle.com*, January 4, 2008.

BELOW RIGHT: Nick Anderson, *Houston Chronicle*, December 5, 2007.

The 2008 presidential campaign would prove to be one of the nation's most historic. The race got off to an early start in January 2007 when Senator Hillary Clinton announced her candidacy. Barack Obama, the freshman senator from Illinois, soon followed. Although other hopefuls stumped through Iowa and New Hampshire, the choice quickly narrowed down to a hotly contested race between a white woman and a black man. By late May, Clinton's "inevitability" factor waned as Obama, already the media's darling, picked up the delegates he needed to sew up the Democratic Party

ABOVE: Michael Ramirez, *Investor's Business Daily*, January 18, 2007.

RIGHT: David Horsey, *Seattle Post-Intelligencer*, August 15, 2008.

nomination. The issue of race was on everyone's mind.

Was America ready to elect a president with a white mother, a black father, and Hussein as a middle name? Speculation about which lever white Americans would pull in the privacy of the voting booths enlivened columns, cartoons, and dinner parties.

ABOVE: Daryl Cagle, *cagle.com*. August 30, 2008.

ABOVE LEFT: Matt Davies, *The Journal News*, New York, March 8, 2008.
Republican candidate John McCain's Vietnam prisoner of war background is juxtaposed with his support of the "Bush war" in Iraq.

BELOW LEFT: Matt Davies, *The Journal News*, New York, August 31, 2008.

Senator John McCain quickly wrapped up the Republican nod, but cartoonists found little humor in his campaign. When dealing with a Vietnam War hero and a former prisoner of war, they were well advised to tread softly. Then at the Republican Convention in St. Paul, Minnesota, McCain surprised everyone by naming Sarah Palin, the governor of Alaska and a self-proclaimed hockey mom, as his running mate. Cartoonists were elated.

The 2008 presidential contest was decided by the time the polls closed on the east coast. When Pennsylvania's and Ohio's electoral votes showed up in the Democrat's column, everyone knew that Barack Hussein Obama would be the 44th President of the United States, and the first African American elected to the nation's highest office. A generation ago, few—black or white—would have dreamed they would live to see such an event.

Many cartoonists chose the Lincoln Memorial as the setting to commemorate Obama's victory. Wasn't it appropriate to return to this site where, in 1963, Martin Luther King, Jr. had declared "I Have a Dream?" The nation's history, good and bad, seemed to be bound up in that statue of ol' Abe high up on that pedestal surveying the country he had fought to hold together.

Joel Pett, *Lexington Herald-Leader*, November 5, 2008.

LEFT: Signe Wilkinson, *Philadelphia Daily News*, March 21, 2008.
Wilkinson's cartoon nailed the nation's discomfort in talking about race.

Clay Bennett, *Chattanooga Times Free Press*, November 5, 2008.

The political cartoon is the embodiment of the American form of government. Democracy is fed by encouraging a free forum for discussion. Wrote historian Larry Mintz, "It takes a confident and aggressive society to consider its most serious problems and reduce them to jokes. It involves a willingness to consider the stupidities and errors of one's environment as less threatening—as, in fact, survivable."

In 1866 *The Nation* magazine concluded, "Humor is not usually a quality of virtuous indignation; and great immoralities, public or private, are not dealt with in a spirit of levity, because to subject them to the ordeal of ridicule would be really to diminish the abhorrence with which they would be regarded." The illustrious journal was mistaken. Americans not only have the capacity to poke fun at their politics and their politicians, but they have done it exceedingly well. Moreover, it has been therapeutic.

Cartoonist C.D. Batchelor believed that "a political cartoonist should have in him a little of the clown, the poet, the historian, the artist and the dreamer." It is a rare amalgam, not one for which the formula is known. As the *Chicago Daily News*' Frederick Richardson remarked at the turn of the twentieth century about the cartoonist, "It is lucky for him that he is born and not made, for the making would be a laborious process."

When Jim Borgman joined the stampede of cartoonists who had either voluntarily or involuntarily relinquished their drawing boards in September 2008, he wrote a letter to his readers at the *Cincinnati Enquirer* that sums up most editorial cartoonists' love affair and dedication to their craft: "I've said my piece, as Grandma Borgman would have said. One week after graduating from college 32 years ago I started drawing editorial cartoons for the *Cincinnati Enquirer*.... I've barely looked up since. Some employee! Not a single promotion in three decades. My buddy says I'm 'still stuck in the same dead-end job' I got right out of college... But what a job. And what a remarkable landscape of nonsense and characters I've gotten to chronicle in the years since. Hidden behind each day's cartoon has been a sweat feast aimed at amusing and engaging you in the topics of our times, all done in the belief that when we are fully immersed in lively debate we make wiser decisions about our world. I've poured my blood and bones into a job which, if done well, looks effortless and whimsical. I've had fun and you've told me you have, too.... There is no place I would have rather invested my life.... I don't know if I'll miss this precious real estate I've enjoyed and the chance to talk about anything on my mind. Sometimes lately when I watch the news I feel like a butcher looking at a field full of cows. I don't see the animals anymore, just the hamburger... Meanwhile, thank you for humoring me. What a pleasure it has been!"

When Joseph Keppler started his magazine *Puck* in 1876, he chose the line for his masthead from Shakespeare: "What fools these mortals be!" As long as mortals continue to be fools, there will be cartoonists.

EPILOGUE

Since 1996, editorial cartooning has lost some of its most venerated practitioners. The Washington Post's Herb Block, who reigned for decades as the dean of political cartoonists, died in 2001. Everyone was astonished to discover that Block left $50 million to create the Herb Block Foundation with a mandate to combat discrimination, prejudices, and abuse by the powerful. Bill Mauldin, died in 2003 after battling Alzheimer's disease, but not before a score of vets who saw themselves reflected in Mauldin's iconic World War II characters, Willie and Joe, showed up at his bedside to honor him. One veteran took the medal off his chest and pinned it on Mauldin's pajamas. Thousands more sent notes. All vividly remembered the impact Mauldin's cartoons had had on them as GIs. David Levine, America's most brilliant caricaturist, died in 2009 having contributed over 3800 drawings to *The New York Review of Books*. Three-time Pulitzer Prize winner, Paul Conrad, who reigned and railed for nearly sixty years at *The Denver Post*, *The Los Angeles Times*, and in syndication died in 2010.

Cartooning's next generation was diminished by the deaths of Jeff MacNelly, the Chicago Tribune's cartoonist, in 2000, and Doug Marlette in 2007. Marlette's outspoken point of view took him to the drawing boards of the Charlotte Observer, Atlanta Journal-Constitution, New York Newsday, Tallahassee Democrat, and Tulsa World.

The work of many cartoonists is preserved in libraries and universities throughout the country. The Library of Congress—by far the largest archive of both historic and current editorial cartoons—received 14,000 of Herb Block's original cartoons, 45,000 sketches and notes, and the funds to catalog and scan his generous legacy. Over 1700 of Bill Mauldin's drawings are also archived there as well as many of his personal papers. The Library of Congress has put 10,000 of its 128,000 cartoons online and the number keeps growing. Ohio State University's Cartoon Research Library, the most comprehensive academic research facility documenting printed cartoon art, has more then 40,000 political cartoons in its database. Major cartooning websites, such as *editorialcartoonists.com*, the Association of American Editorial Cartoonists official website, *cagle.com*, and *gocomics.com*, as well as individual newspapers' and cartoonists' sites, offer a roundup of hundreds of new cartoons each morning, featuring local, national, and international issues. Today's cartoons can be viewed on the Internet 24/7 and may be seen by millions around the world.

ACKNOWLEDGMENTS

This book is built on two previous publications. *The Ungentlemanly Art: A History of American Political Cartoons* by Stephen Hess and Milton Kaplan, published by Macmillan Publishing Co. in 1968 was the first. (Mr. Kaplan, the Specialist in Historical Prints at the Library of Congress died in 1988. We thank his family, Stanley and Doris Kaplan and their daughters Gail and Linda, for their ongoing support of subsequent publications.) Over the next thirty years political cartoons were the subject of increasing interest. Scholars and laymen alike added to the knowledge and critical dialogue on the role of the political cartoon in American society. *Drawn & Quartered; The History of American Political Cartoons*, an updated version of the previous work, written by Stephen Hess and Sandy Northrop and published by Elliott & Clark Publishing in 1996 grew out of this new interest.

Richard Samuel West elevated writing on the political cartoon to a new level of inquiry. As the editor of two journals, *The Puck Papers* and *Target*, he offered an important avenue for expanding commentary and scholarship. West shared his private library and his knowledge with the authors.

The late Draper Hill, regarded by many as the most knowledgeable scholar on political cartooning and the cartoonist for the *Detroit News*, assisted Hess and Kaplan in the first edition. He also generously contributed his time to the original edition of *Drawn and Quartered.* Roger Fischer, professor of American history at the University of Minnesota, Duluth, provided a fresh eye and dry wit.

The book would not have been possible without the assistance of many people at the Library of Congress: Bernard Reilly and Harry Katz, former curatorial heads, Prints and Photographs; Sara Duke; and the staff at the Prints and Photographs reading room. Ms. Duke, who is now Curator, Popular & Applied Graphic Art, read and commented on the manuscript.

The late Doug Marlette was the first of many cartoonists to take the time to share his thoughts on political cartooning with the authors. Jules Feiffer and Kevin Kallaugher also graciously contributed their insights.

To these individuals and many more who have patiently answered questions, lent their ears and their opinions as the new edition was being prepared, we offer our thanks, especially Sarah Chilton at the Brookings Library, and Juanett T. Davis and Matthew Waring for their unflagging assistance.

Our deepest thanks to Carl Northrop. Whether related or not, he has been our dedicated counselor and has traveled with us through each edition of this book.

And finally, our thanks to our patient friends and caring collaborators at Transaction Publishers: Irving Louis Horowitz, Mary Curtis, Maureen Feldman, Andrew McIntosh and Tim Conboy.

RESOURCES

Political cartoons have come under scrutiny as subjects for scholarly study thanks to many major institutions. The Library of Congress Print and Photographs division is the largest and most important archive and continues to expand its holdings. In 2001, the acquisition of the Art Wood Collection of Caricature and Cartoon containing 36,000 images more than doubled its size.

Ohio State University's Cartoon Research Library, headed by Lucy Shelton Casewell, is also a major resource on comic art. In 2008, the collection of Mort Walker, formerly housed at the The International Museum of Cartoon Art in Boca Raton, Florida was added to its holdings. A Festival of Cartoon Art focusing on a key aspect of cartooning is held triennially on the Ohio State campus.

Other organizations are dedicated to preserving and exhibiting the best of the profession. The Cartoon Art Museum in San Francisco opened to the public in 1987.

Journals such as *Target (1981-87)*, edited by Richard Samuel West, have offered forums for interviews with practicing cartoonists, articles on the profession's rich history, and commentary on the health of the craft. *Inks, Cartoon and Comic Art Studies*, published by Ohio State University, carried on West's outstanding tradition from 1994-1997.

The following bibliography is broken down by chapter. Although collections of cartoonists' work have not been included, they are an enjoyable and important primary source. Websites devoted to the study of comic art and editorial cartoons have also proliferated.

General Books and Articles on Caricature and Political Cartoons

Amon Carter Museum of Western Art. *The Image of America in Caricature and Cartoon.* Fort Worth: The Museum, 1976.

"The Art of Political Cartoons." *The Living Age,* April 24, 1920.

"The Artist as a Social Critic." *Print,* January-February, 1966.

Ashbee, C. R. *Caricature.* London: Chapman and Hall, 1928.

Becker, Stephen. *Comic Art in America.* New York: Simon and Schuster, 1959.

Blaisdell, Thomas C., Jr., Peter Selz. *The American Presidency in Political Cartoons: 1776—1976.* Santa Barbara: Peregrine Smith, 1976.

Blunt, Abbot. "Roland C. (Doc) Bowman." *The American Cartoonist, August* 1903.

Bredhoff, Stacey. *Draw! Political Cartoons from Left to*

Right. Washington, D.C.: National Archives, 1991. (Catalogue for the National Archives and Records exhibition celebrating the 200th anniversary of the Bill of Rights—June 14, 1991-August 1992.)

Bruckner, D. J. R., Seymour Chwast, and Steven Heller. *Art Against War: 400 Years of Protest in Art.* New York: Abbeville Press, 1984.

Catalogue of the Salon of American Humorists, A Political and Social Pageant from the Revolution to the Present Day. New York: College Art Association, 1933.

Coupe, W A. "Observations on a Theory of Political Caricature." *Comparative Studies in Society and History,* vol. 11, January 1969.

Craven, Thomas, ed. *Cartoon Cavalcade.* New York: Simon and Schuster, 1943.

Cuff, Roger Penn. "The American Editorial Cartoon—A Critical Historical Sketch." *The Journal of Educational Sociology,* October 1945.

Deur, Lynne. *Political Cartoonists.* Minneapolis: Lerner Publications Company, 1972.

Emory, Michael and Edwin. *The Press and America, An Interpretive History of the Mass Media,* rev. ed. Englewood Cliffs, N.J.: Prentice Hall, 1988.

Feaver, William. *Masters of Caricature.* New York: Alfred A. Knopf, 1981.

Fischer, Roger. *Them Damned Pictures: Explorations in American Political Cartoon Art.* North Haven, Conn.: Shoe String Press, 1996.

Geipel, John. *The Cartoon: A Short History of Graphic Comedy and Satire.* New York: A.S. Barnes and Co., 1972.

Getlein, Frank and Dorothy. *The Bite of the Print: Satire and Irony in Woodcuts, Engravings, Etchings, Lithographs, and Serigraphs.* New York: C.N. Potter, 1963.

Gombrich, Ernest H. *Art and Illusion: A Study in the Psychology of Pictorial Representation,* rev. ed. Princeton: Princeton University Press, 1969.

___, and Ernst Kris. *Caricature.* London:King Penguin, 1940.

___. "The Experiment of Caricature." In *Art and Illusion.* London: Phaidon, 1963.

___. "The Cartoonist's Armory." In *Meditations on a Hobby Horse.* London: Phaidon, 1963.

Heller, Steven, and Gail Anderson. *The Savage Mirror, The Art of Contemporary Caricature.* New York: Watson-Guptill, 1992.

Hesse, Don. "The Ungentlemanly Art." *The Quill,* December 1959.

Hoff, Syd. *Editorial and Political Cartooning from Earliest Times to Present.* New York: Stravon Educational Press, 1976.

Inge, Thomas. *Comics as Culture.* Jackson: University Press of Mississippi, 1990.

Johnson, Gerald W. *The Lines Are Drawn.* Philadelphia: Lippincott, 1958.

Leonard, Thomas C. *The Power of the Press, The Birth of American Political Reporting.* New York: Oxford University Press, 1986.

Marzio, Peter. *The Men and Machines of American Journalism.* Washington, D.C.: National Museum of History and Technology, Smithsonian Institution, 1973. (A pictorial essay from the Henry R. Luce Hall of News Reporting.)

Maurice, Arthur Bartlett, and Frederic Taber Cooper. *History of the Nineteenth Century in Caricature.* New York: Dodd, Mead, 1904.

Maurice, Arthur Bartlett, ed. "Cartoons That Have Swayed History." *The Mentor,* July 1930.

Mitchell, John Ames. "Contemporary American Caricature." *Scribner's Magazine,* December 1889.

Mott, Frank Luther. *American Journalism.* New York, 1950.

___. *The History of American Journalism.* New York: Macmillan, 1972.

___. *A History of American Magazines.* 4 vols.

Cambridge: Harvard University Press, 1938—57.

Murrell, William. *A History of American Graphic Humor.* 2 vols. New York: Cooper Square Publishers, 1967.

Nevins, Allan, and Frank Weitenkampf. *A Century of Political Cartoons: Caricature in the United States from 1800 to 1900.* New York: Charles Scribner's Sons, 1944.

Payne, Harold. "Our Caricaturists and Cartoonists." *Munsey's Magazine,* February 1894.

Philippe, Robert. *Political Graphics, Art as a Weapon.* New York: Abbeville Press, 1980.

Press, Charles. *The Political Cartoon.* East Brunswick, N.J.: Associated University Presses, 1981.

Reilly, Bernard. *American Political Prints, 1766-1876: A Catalog of the Collections in the Library of Congress.* Boston: G.K. Hall, 1991.

___. Introduction to "In Good Conscience: The Radical Tradition in 20th Century American Illustration." Katonah, N.Y.: Katonah Museum of Art, 1992.

Shelton, William Henry. "The Comic Paper in America." *The Critic,* September 1901.

Sheridan, Martin. *Comics and Their Creators: Life Stories of American Cartoonists.* Hale, Cushman and Flint, 1942.

Shikes, Ralph E. *The Indignant Eye: The Artist as Social Critic in Prints and Drawings from the Fifteenth Century to Picasso.* Boston: Beacon Press, 1969.

___, and Steven Heller. *The Art of Satire: Painters as Caricaturists and Cartoonists from Delacroix to Picasso.* New York: Horizon Press, 1984.

Smith, Henry Ladd. "The Rise and Fall of the Political Cartoon." *Saturday Review,* May 29, 1954.

Smith, Katherine Louise. "Newspaper Art and Artists." *The*

Bookman, August 1901.

Teppel, John. *The Media in America.* Thomas Crowell Co., 1978.

Trumble, Alfred. "Satire, With Crayon and Pen." *The Epoch,* June 13, 1890.

Weaver, John D. "Drawing Blood: Political Cartoonists." *Holiday,* August 1915.

Weitenkampf, Frank. "American Cartoonists of Today." *Century,* February 1913.

___. *American Graphic Art.* New York: Macmillan, 1924.

___. *Manhattan Kaleidoscope.* New York: Charles Scribner's Sons, 1947.

___. *Political Caricature in the United States in Separately Published Cartoons.* New York: New York Public Library Bulletin, 1953.

Whitaker, J. V. "American Caricature." *Leisure Hour,* September 30, October 21, November 25, and December 16, 1876.

White, Frank Linstow. "Some American Caricaturists." *The Journalist,* November 19, 1887.

White, Richard Grant. "Caricature and Caricaturists." *Harper's Monthly Magazine,* April 1862.

Wood, Art. *Great Cartoonists and Their Art.* Gretna, LA: Pelican Publishing, 1987.

Wright, Grant. *The Art of Caricature.* New York: Baker Taylor, 1904.

Chapter One

Appel, John and Selma. "The Grand Old Sport of Hating Catholics: American Anti-Catholic Caricature Prints." *The Critic,* November-December 1971.

___. "From Shanties to Lace Curtains: The Irish Image in *Puck,* 1876-1910." *Comparative Studies in Society and History,* vol. 12, October 1971.

___. *Jews in American Graphic Satire and Humor.* Cincinnati: American Jewish Archives, 1984.

___. *Patriots to Patriots: American Irish in Caricature and Comic Art.* East Lansing: Michigan State University Museum, 1990.

Astor, David. "Black Progress in Comics." *Editor and Publisher,* February 4, 1984.

Horn, Maurice. *In the Eye of the Beholder. Contemporary Issues in Stereotyping.* New York: Praeger, 1982.

Ohio State University Libraries. *Cartoons and Ethnicity.* Columbus: Ohio State University, 1992. (A catalogue accompanying an exhibit for the 1992 Festival of Cartoon Art.)

West, Richard Samuel. "The Pen and the Parrot, Charles Nelan Takes on the Governor of Pennsylvania." *Target,* vol. 5, no. 21 (Autumn 1986): 4-11.

Chapter Two

Aquila, Dani, ed. *Taking Liberty with the Lady.* Nashville: Eagle Nest Publishing, 1986.

Beardsley, William A. *An Old New Haven Engraver and His Work: Amos Doolittle.* 1910. (Photostat in the Library of Congress.)

Bishop, Joseph Bucklin. "Early Political Caricature in America." *Century,* June 1892.

Browne, Ray B., Marshall W Fishwick, and Kevin O. Browne. *Dominant Symbols in Popular Culture.* Bowling Green: Bowling Green State University Popular Press, 1990.

Cawelti, John G. "Symbols of Ethnicity and Popular Culture." In *Dominant Symbols in Popular Culture.* Bowling Green: Bowling Green State University Popular Press, 1990.

Grouse, Russell. *Mr. Currier and Mr. Ives.* Garden City, N.Y: Doubleday, Doran, 1930.

Cunningham, Noble. *The Image of Thomas Jefferson in the Public Eye.* Charlottesville: University of Virginia Press, 1981.

___. *Popular Images of the Presidency from Washington to Lincoln.* Charlottesville: University of Virginia Press, 1988.

Davidson, Nancy R. "Andrew Jackson in Cartoon and Caricature." In *American Printmaking before 1876: Fact, Fiction and Fantasy.* (Papers presented at a symposium held at Library of Congress, June 12 and 13, 1972.) Washington, D.C.: Library of Congress, 1975.

Fischer, Roger. "Not Yet an Icon: Liberty in Cartoon 1879-1886." *Target,* vol. 5, no. 20 (Autumn 1985): 4-11.

___. "Political Cartoon Symbols and the Divergence of Popular and Traditional Cultures in the United States." In *Dominant Symbols in Popular Culture.* Bowling Green: Bowling Green State University Popular Press, 1990.

Hammer, Mrs. D. Harry. "Cartoons of Uncle Sam." *Cartoon,* July 1913.

___. "The Translators of Uncle Sam." *Cartoon,* June 1913.

Harwell, Richard Barksdale. "Confederate Anti-Lincoln Literature." *Lincoln Herald,* Fall 1951.

Hill, Draper. *Fashionable Contrasts, Caricatures by James Gillray.* London: Phaidon, 1966.

___. *Mr. Gillray, The Caricaturist.* London: Phaidon, 1965.

Jones, Michael Wynn. *The Cartoon History of the American Revolution.* New York: Putnam, 1975.

Ketchum, Alton. *Uncle Sam: The Man and the Legend.* New York: Hill and Wang, 1959.

Lee, James Melvin. "Lincoln as *Vanity Fair* Saw Him." *Cartoon,* February 1916.

___. "Punchinello and Its Cartoons." *Cartoon,* August 1916.

Mattern, Kendall B., Jr. "The Birth and Long Life of Uncle Sam." *Target,* vol. 1, no. 3. (Spring 1982): 15-19.

___. "Where Cartoonists Hawked Their Wares." *Target,* vol. 2, no. 8 (Summer 1983): 11-15.

___. "Cartoonist for the Lost Cause." *Target,* vol. 4, no. 16 (Summer 1985): 4-9.

Morse, John D., ed. *Prints in and of America to 1850.* Charlottesville: University of Virginia Press, 1970.

Murrell, William. "Rise and Fall of Cartoon Symbols," *American Scholar,* Summer 1935.

Olson, Lester. *Emblems of American Community in the Revolutionary Era.* Washington, D.C.: Smithsonian Institution, 1991.

Peters, Harry T *Currier and Ives, Printmakers to the American People.* 2 vols. Garden City, N.Y.: Doubleday, Doran, 1929 and 1931.

Ricker, Mary Swing. "'Uncle Sam' in Cartoon." *The World Today,* October 1910.

Riley, Sam G. "Symbolism in Humor." In *Dominant Symbols in Popular Culture.* Bowling Green: Bowling Green University Popular Press, 1990.

Shaw, Albert. *Abraham Lincoln.* 2 vols. New York: Review of Reviews, 1929.

Volck, A. J. "Confederate War Etchings." *The Magazine of History,* extra no. 60, 1917.

Walsh, William S. *Abraham Lincoln and the London Punch.* New York: Moffat, Yard, 1909.

Wechsler, Judith. *A Human Comedy: Physiognomy and Caricature in 19th Century Paris.* London: Thames and Hudson, 1982.

Wilson, Rufus Rockwell. *Lincoln in Caricature.* New York: Horizon, 1953.

Chapter Three

Hill, Draper. "'What Fools These Mortals Be!' A Study of the Work of Joseph Keppler—Founder of *Puck.*" B.A. Thesis, Harvard College, 1957.

Keller, Morton. *The Art and Politics of Thomas Nast.* New York: Oxford University Press, 1968.

Maurice, Arthur Bartlett. "Thomas Nast and His Cartoons." *The Bookman,* March 1902.

Paine, Albert Bigelow. *Thomas Nast, His Period and His Pictures.* New York: Harper, 1904.

St. Hill, Thomas Nast. *Thomas Nast Cartoons and Illustrations.* New York: Dover, 1974.

West, Richard Samuel. *Satire on Stone: The Political Cartoons of Joseph Keppler.* Urbana: University of Illinois Press, 1988.

Chapter Four

Abbott, Lyman. "Cartoons and Caricatures in War Time." *The Outlook,* November 8, 1916.

Ade, George. *Chicago.* Chicago: Henry Regnery, 1963.

___. "March Fourth in Musslewhite." *Collier's,* March 1913.

Blackbeard, Bill, ed. *R. F. Outcault's The Yellow Kid.* Northampton, Mass.: Kitchen Sink Press, 1995.

Cartoons of the War in 1898 with Spain. Chicago: Belford, Middlebrook, 1898.

Casewell, Lucy Shelton. "Seven Cartoonists," *1989 Festival of Cartoon Art Catalogue,* Columbus: Ohio State University, 1989.

___. "Edwinna Dunn: Pioneer Woman Editorial Cartoonist: 1915—1917." *Journalism History,* vol. 15, no. 1 (Spring 1988): 2-7.

Chicago Tribune Co. *The Chicago Tribune: The Rise of a Great American Newspaper.* Chicago: Chicago Tribune Co., 1986.

___. *The Chicago Tribune, WGN.* Chicago: Chicago Tribune Co., 1922.

Davenport, Homer. *Cartoons.* New York: DeWitt, 1898.

___. *The Dollar or the Man?* Boston: Small Maynard, 1900.

___. "The Gentle Art of Making the Wicked Squirm." *New York Journal,* April 16, 1899.

___. "The Personal Narrative of Homer Davenport." *The Pacific Monthly,* November and December 1905.

___. *My Quest of the Arab Horse.* New York: Dodge, 1909.

Eastman, Max.. *Journalism Versus Art.* New York: Alfred A. Knopf, 1916.

Fitzgerald, Richard. *Art and Politics: Cartoonists of the Masses and Liberator.* Westport, Conn.: Greenwood Press, 1973.

Franzen, Monika, and Nancy Ethiel. *Make Way! 200 Years of American Women in Cartoons.* Chicago: Chicago Review Press, 1988.

Goodrich, Lloyd. *John Sloan.* New York: Macmillan, 1952.

Hecht, George. "How the Cartoonist Can Help Win the War." *Cartoon,* February 1918.

___. *The War in Cartoons.* New York: Button, 1919.

"Historical Campaign Caricatures." *The World's Work* November 1900.

Marschall, Richard. "Richard Outcault." In *America's Great Comic Strip Artists.* New York: Abbeville Press, 1989: 19-40.

McCutcheon, John T. *Teddy Roosevelt in Cartoons.* New York: McClure, 1910.

___. *Drawn From Memory: The Autobiography of John T. McCutcheon.* New York, Indianapolis: Bobbs-Merrill, 1950.

Nelan, Charles. *Cartoons of Our War with Spain.* New York: Stokes, 1898.

North, Joseph. *Robert Minor, Artist and Crusader, An Informal Biography.* New York: New York International Publishers, 1956.

O'Neill, William L, ed. *Echoes of Revolt, The Masses 1911-1917.* Chicago: Quadrangle Books, 1966.

Opper, Frederick. *Willie and His Papa.* New York: Grosset & Dunlap, 1901.

Raemaekers, Louis. *America in the War.* New York: Century, 1918.

___. *Kultur in Cartoons.* New York: Century, 1917.

___. *Raemaekers' Cartoon History of the War.* New York: Century, 1918.

___. *Raemaekers' Cartoons.* Garden City, N.Y.: Doubleday, 1917.

Robinson, Boardman. *Cartoons on the War.* New York: Dutton, 1915.

___. "America's Foremost Cartoonist Talks on

Our Cartooning Art, and Tells Why It Misses Being Great." *Pep,* November 1917.

___. *Ninety- Three Drawings.* Colorado Springs: Fine Arts Center, 1937.

Roosevelt, Theodore. "The Genius of Raemaekers." *Land and Water,* June 7,1917.

Rutledge, William A., III. "Dean of American Cartoonists [JohnT. McCutcheon]," *The Quill,* June 1939.

Sasowsky, Norman. *Reginald Marsh.* New York: Praeger, 1956.

Shaw, Albert. *A Cartoon History of Roosevelt's Career.* New York: Review of Reviews, 1910.

Spencer, Dick, III. "The Femme and the Pen." *Editorial Cartooning.* Ames: Iowa State College Press, 1949.

Westerman, Harry J. "Outlines Career of R.F. Outcault, Ohio-Born Artist." *The Ohio Newspaper,* December 1933.

Widney, Gustavus C. "John McCutcheon, Cartoonist." *The World Today, July—December* 1908.

Young, Art. *Art Young, His Life and Times.* New York: Sheridan House, 1939; Westport, Conn.: Hyperion Press, 1975.

___. *The Best of Art Young.* New York: Vanguard, 1936.

___. *On My Way.* New York: Liveright, 1928.

Zurrier, Rebecca. *Art for The Masses.* Philadelphia: Temple University Press, 1988.

Chapter Five

Berryman, Clifford K. *Berryman Cartoons.* Washington, D.C.: Saks & Co., 1900.

___. *Development of the Cartoon.* Columbia: University of Missouri Bulletin, 1926.

___. "Cartoonist to Editor." *The Quill,* October 1951.

___. "Two Blocks in One." *New Republic,* October 13, 1952.

Carnes, Cecil. "Then He Found a Shoe That Fit [Rollin Kirby]." *The Quill,* April 1939.

Darling, Jay N. *As Ding Saw Hoover.* Ames: Iowa State College Press, 1954.

___. *Ding's Half Century.* New York: Duell, Sloan &Pearce, 1962.

Fitzpatrick, Daniel R. *As I Saw It.* New York: Simon and Schuster, 1953.

Johnson, Herbert. *Cartoons by Herbert Johnson.* Philadelphia: Lippincott, 1936.

___."Why Cartoon—And How." *Saturday Evening Post,* July 14, 1928.

Kirby, Rollin. *Highlights, A Cartoon History of the Nineteen Twenties.* New York: Payson, 1931.

___. "My Creed as a Cartoonist." *Pep,* December 1918.

Lorimer, George Horace. *Creating America: George Horace Lorimer and the Saturday Evening Post.* Pittsburgh: University of Pittsburgh Press, 1989.

Mauldin, Bill. *Back Home.* New York: William Sloan Associates, 1947.

___.*The Brass Ring.* New York: WW Norton, 1971.

___. *I've Decided I Want My Seat Back.* New York: Harper and Row, 1965.

___. *A Sort of a Saga.* New York: Sloane, 1949.

___. *Up-Front.* New York: The World Publishing Company, 1945.

___. *What's Got Your Back Up?* New York: Harper, 1961.

"Mauldin: From Willie and Joe to Ronnie." *Target,* vol. 3, no. 10. (Winter 1984): 4-13.

Maurice, Arthur Bartlett. *How They Draw Prohibition.* New York: Association Against the Prohibition Amendment, 1930.

Neuberger, Richard L. "Hooverism in the Funnies." *New Republic,* July 11, 1934.

Rutledge, William A. "The Life Guard and the Lady [Vaughn Shoemaker]." *The Quill,* September 1938.

West, Richard Samuel. "The Politicizing of Ding." *Target,* vol. 1, no. 4 (Summer 1982): 15-19.

___, and Kendall B. Mattern, Jr. "The New Deal in Cartoon." *Target, vol. 2,* no. 5 (Autumn 1982): 14-19.

Chapter Six

Adams, John G. *Without Precedent.* New York: W.W. Norton, 1983.

Bayley, Edwin R. *Joe McCarthy and the Press.* Madison: University of Wisconsin Press, 1981.

Block, Herbert. *Herblock: A Cartoonist's Life.* New York: Macmillan, 1993.

___. *The Herblock Book.* Boston: Beacon Press, 1952.

___. "Herblock on Political Cartooning." *Target,* vol. 4, no. 14 (Winter 1985): 15.

___ *Herblock's Here and Now.* New York: Simon and Schuster, 1955.

"Conrad: Man of Opinion." *Target,* vol. 2, no. 7 (Spring 1983): 4-10.

"A Dancer, Bernard Mergendeiler, and Seven Presidents (An

Interview with Jules Feiffer)." *Target,* vol. 2, no. 6 (Winter 1983): 4-11.

Fischetti, John. *Zinga, Zinga, Za!* Chicago: Follett, 1973.

Harrington, Oliver W., *Bootsie and Others.* New York: Dodd, Mead, 1958.

___.*Where Is the Justice.* Detroit: Walter O. Evans, 1991.

___. *Why I Left America.* Detroit: Walter O. Evans, 1991.

Inge, Thomas. *Dark Laughter: The Satiric Art of Oliver Harrington.* Jackson: University Press of Mississippi, 1993.

"Herblock: The Flame Still Burns Bright." *Target,* vol. 4, no. 14 (Winter 1985): 4-12.

Marschall, Richard. "Walt Kelly." In *Americas Great Comic Strip Artists.* New York: Abbeville Press, 1989: 255-275.

Chapter Seven

Barton, Mary Ann, and Paul C. Barton, eds. *Campaign: A Campaign History of Bill Clinton's Race for the White House.* Fayetteville: University of Arkansas Press, 1993.

"Borgman—In for the Long Haul." *Target,* vol. 4 [5], no. 19 (Spring 1986): 4-15.

"David Levine's Body Count." *Target,* vol. 3, no. 12 (Winter 1984): 4-12.

"Don Wright, Cartooning Journalist." *Target,* vol. 1, no. 1 (Autumn 1981): 4-11.

"Doonesbury: Drawing and Quartering for Fun and Profit." *Time,* February 9, 1976: 57-66.

Grove, Lloyd. "Trudeau!" *Target,* vol. 5 [6], no. 23 (Spring 1987): 13-21.

Judge, Lee and Richard Samuel West. "Why Political Cartoonists Sell Out." *The Washington Monthly,* (September 1988): 38-42.

"MacNelly Returns." *Target,* vol. 1, no. 3 (Spring 1982): 4-12.

"Mark Alan Stamaty—Cartooning on the Edge." *Target,* vol. 5 [6], no. 22 (Winter 1987): 4-12.

Marlette, Doug. *In Your Face, A Cartoonist at Work.* Boston: Houghton Mifflin Company, 1991.

"Politics and Emotion: The Art of Tony Auth." *Target,* vol. 1, no. 2 (Winter 1982): 11-17.

O'Connor, Clint. "Cartoonist Tom Toles: A Quirky Light in the Murk of Politics." *Washington Journalism Review,* December 1988: 24—30.

"Oliphant: Quintessential Cartooning. Part 1." *Target,* vol. 1, no. 4 (Summer 1982): 4-8.

"Oliphant: Quintessential Cartooning. Part 2." *Target,* vol. 2, no. 5 (Autumn 1982): 4-12.

"The Peters Principle: Move the Reader." *Target,* vol. 3, no. 11 (Spring 1984): 4-12.

"Quick Draw: Jeff MacNelly Gives Big Shots the Faces They Deserve." *Washingtonian,* May 1991: 32-39.

Reidelbach, Maria. *Completely Mad: A History of the Comic Book and Magazine.* Boston: Little Brown and Co., 1991.

"Southern Populism-Cartooning by Marlette." *Target,* vol. 5, no. 17 (Autumn 1985): 4-11.

Chapter Eight

Alcaraz, Lalo. *Migra Mouse: Political Cartoons on Immigration.* New York: RDV Books/Akashic Books, 2004.

Bates, Eric. "Doonesbury Goes to War," *Rolling Stone,* August 5, 2004.

Borgman, Jim. "Letter to Readers," *Cincinnati Enquirer,* September 26, 2008.

Brooks, Charles. *Best Editorial Cartoons of the Year, 1997-2008.* Gretna, Louisiana: Pelican Publishing Company.

Campbell, Gordon. "E-mail to Daryl Cagle," *cagle.com,* March 18, 2008.

Campbell, James T. "Excising La Cucaracha no joke for followers of strip," *Houston Chronicle,* September 22, 2007.

DePastino, Todd. *Bill Mauldin: A Life Up Front.* New York: W.W. Norton & Company, 2008.

"Drawing Fire: The State of Political Cartooning." American Press Institute: J. Montgomery Curtis Memorial Seminar, 1998.

"Editorial Cartoons: The Impact and Issues of an Evolving Craft," *Nieman Reports*, Winter 2004.

Horsey, David. *Draw Quick, Shoot Straight, Seattle Post-Intelligenceri,* 2007.

Lamb, Christopher. *Drawn to Extremes: The Use and Abuse of Editorial Cartoons*. New York: Columbia University Press, 2004.

Lamb, Christopher. "Editorial Cartooning: Tradition, Timidity and Transition," *Nieman Reports*, Fall 2008.

Rall, Ted. *Attitude: The New Subversive Political Cartoonists.* New York: Nantier, Beall, Minoustchine, 2002.

Telnaes, Ann. *Humor's Edge.* San Francisco: Pomegranate Press, 2004.

"The State of Editorial Cartooning," *Political Science and Politics*, April 2007.

Trudeau, G.B. *The Long Road Home*. Kansas City: Andrews McMeel Publishing, 2005.

ILLUSTRATION SOURCES AND COPYRIGHTS

Please note: All illustrations from the Prints and Photographs Division, Library of Congress, use the prefix LC-USZ62 unless otherwise noted. The prefix has been shortened to "LC" within the source listing. Library of Congress numbers are provided whenever known, although the authors may have secured the art from other sources.

2: © Christian Science Monitor; **6:** *Life,* Volume XLIX, No 1269, p.274-275; **8:** LC 22116; **9:** LC 34200; **11 L:** Courtesy Bill Mauldin. *Up Front,* New York: W.W Norton and Co. 1991, p. 133; **11 R:** *HerblockA Cartoonist's Life,* New York: Macmillan, 1993, p.144; **12:** Lyndon Baines Johnson Library, National Archives; **13 L:** LC 40042; **13 R:** Victoria Schuck Collection, John F. Kennedy Library, National Archives; **14 R:** Mike Peters, © 1980 *Dayton Daily News. On the Edge,* Dayton: DNI Publishing, 1994, p.32; **15 L:** ©Tony Auth. Reprinted by permission of Universal Press Syndicate. *Behind the Lines,* Boston: Houghton Mifflin Co., 1977; **15 R:** Richard Samuel West Collection; **16 L:** *Life,* Volume 66, No 1724, p.898; **16 R:** © *Arkansas Democrat Gazette. God Would Have Done It if He'd Had the Money,* Little Rock: Arkansas Wildlife Federation Conservation Foundation, 1983; **17:** *Bootsie and Others,* New York: Dodd, Mead, 1958; **18 L:** LC 324. **18R:** LC 2176; **19 L:** Richard Samuel West Collection; **19R:** LC 34327; **20 L:** LC 34262; **20 C:** Dennis Ryan Collection; **20 R:** *Herblock: A Cartoonist's Life.* New York: Macmillan, 1993, p.108; **21 U:** © Pat Oliphant. Courtesy Susan Conway Gallery; **21 L:** © Christian Science Monitor. *What, Me Incumbent?,* Boston: The Christian Science Publishing Society, 1992; **22 L:** LC 773; **22 R:** LC 34218; **23:** © 1982 *Los Angeles Times.* Distributed by *Los Angeles Times* Syndicate. Reprinted wirh permission. *Conartist,* Los Angeles; *Los Angeles Times,* 1993, p.91; **24:** LC 9701; **25 L:** Historical Society of Pennsylvania; **25 R:** LC 1531; **26:** LC 1985; **27 UL:** LC 1979; **27 LL:** LC 16780; **27 R:** Reprinted with permission Cartoonists and Writers Syndicate; **28 L:** LC 65329; **28 R:** American Antiquarian Society, Worcester, MA; **29 L:** LC 65329; **29 R:** LC 1569; **30 L:** Richard Samuel West Collection, LC 34211; **30 R:** LC 12025; **31 UL:** LC 8278; **31 LL:** © Tony Auth. Reprinted by permission of Universal Press Syndicare, *Behind the Lines,* Boston: Houghton Mifflin Co., 1977; **31 LR:** © Christian Science Monitor; **32 L, 32 C, and 32 R:** *Taking Liberty with the Lady,* Nashville: Eagle Nest Publishing, 1986, p.99, 23, 26; **33 UL:** © 1980 Doug Marlette. *Drawing Blood,* Washington: Graphic Press, 1980, p. 10; **33 LL:** © Signe Wilkinson. Reprinted with permission Cartoonists and Writers Syndicate. *Taking Liberty with the Lady,* Nashville: Eagle Nest Publishing, 1986, p. 104; **33 R:** *Taking Liberty with the Lady,* Nashville: Eagle Nest Publishing, 1986, p.92; **34 L:** © 1991 Jim Borgman. Reprinted with special permission of King Features Syndicate. *Disturbing the Peace,* Cincinnati: Colloquial Books, 1995, p.37; **34 R:** LC 44199; **35 L:** LC 100132; **35 R:** © Draper Hill. *Detroit News. Political Asylum,* Windsor, Ontario: Art Gallery of Windsor, 1985, p.9; **36 L:** LC 34226; 37: Collection of the New York Historical Society; **38:** LC 24865; **39L:** Collection of the Library Company of Philadelphia; **39 R:** Collection of the Boston Public Library, Print Department; **40 R:** LC 1582; **41 L:** LC 1562; **41 R:** Courtesy Edward Sorel. *Superpen,* New York: Random House, 1978; **42 R:** LC 2068; **43:** LC 1990; **44:** LC 9648; **44 LL:** LC 10559; **44 LR:** LC 763; **45 L:** LC 1969; **45 R:** LC 12425; **46** and **47L:** Richard Samuel West Collection; **47 R:** LC 34324; **48:** Richard Samuel West Collection; **49 L:** LC 6860; **49 R:** LC 786; **50 L and 50 R:** Richard Samuel West Collection; **51:** Richard Samuel West Collection, LC 34232; **52 and 53 L:** Author's Collection; **53 R:** LC 34233; **54 L, R, 55, 56, 57 L, R, 58L:** Author's Collection; **58 R:** Richard Samuel West Collection, LC 34238; **59 L:** Richard Samuel West Collection; **59 R:** Richard Samuel West Collection, LC 34239; **60 and 61:** *Satire in Stone,* Chicago: University of Illinois Press, 1988, p.169 and 356; **62:** LC 34249; **63 U:** Richard Samuel West Collection, LC 27761; **63 L:** © 1987 *Los Angeles Times.* Distributed by *Los Angeles Times* Syndicate. Reprinted with permission, *Conartist,* Los Angeles: *Los Angeles Times,* 1993, p.127; **64 L:** LC 34249; **64 R:** LC 34248; **65 U:** *Life,* Volume XXVII. No 694; **65:** *Life,* Volume XXVII. No 699; **66:** *Satire in Stone,* Chicago: University of Illinois Press, 1988, p.401; **67:** LC 34237; **68:** LC 53751; **71 L:** Collection, San Francisco Academy of Comic Art; **71 UR:** LC 34261; **71 LR:** *Inks: Cartoon and Comic Studies,* Vol 2, No 2, May 1995, p. 15; **72:** LC 34268; **73 L:** Richard Samuel West Collection, LC 797; **73 R:** *Inks: Cartoon and Comic Studies,* Vol 2, No 2, May 1995, p.3; **74 UL:** LC 34264; **74 UR:** LC 34266; **75:** LC 34268; **76 L:** LC 34281; **76 C:** LC 34282; **76 R:** LC 34284; **77:** *Drawn From Memory,* Indianapolis: Bobbs-Merrill Co., Inc., 1950, cover; **78 U:** Richard Samuel West Collection; **78 L:** Authors Collection; **79 L:** LC 34276; **79 UR:** *The American Presidency in Political Cartoons: 1776-1976,* Santa Barbara: Peregrine Smith, Inc., 1976, p.151; **79 LR:** LC 34273; **80 R:** Reprinted in *Cartoons Magazine,* January 1912; **81:** LC 111306, Godstein Collection; **82 L:** National Archives; **83:** Richard Samuel West Collection *(Great War in* London: Fine Art Society, 1917); **84 UL:** Richard Samuel West Collection; **84 LL:** *The Gibson Girl and Her America,* New York: Dover, 1969, p.92; **84 R:** Richard Samuel West Collection; **85 L:** *Echoes of Revolt: The Masses 1911-1916,* Chicago: Ivan R. Dee, Inc., 1989, p.242; **85 R:** Richard Samuel West Collection, LC 34294; **87 R:** Richard Samuel West Collection; **88 L:** Granger Collection; **88 R:** State Historical Society of Missouri, Columbia; **89 L:** Richard Samuel West Collection; **90 L:** LC 34303; **90 R:** LC 34304; **91:** *Life,*.VO LX, NO 1563. *Make Way: 200 Years of American Women in Cartoons,* Chicago Review Press, 1988, cover; **92 UL:** Library of Congress; **92 LL:** LC 34336; 92 R: LC 14232; 93 L: Library of Congress; **93 R:** The Schomburg Center for Research in Black Culture. Scrapbook Collection. New York Public Library; **94:** © Patricia Arno. Peter Arno Cartoon. Used by Permission. Franklin D. Roosevelt Library, National Archives; **95 L:** LC 34343; **95 UR:** Library of Congress; **96 L:** Franklin D. Roosevelt Library, National Archives; **96 R:** *The American Presidency in Political Cartoons, 1776-1976,* Santa Barbara: Peregrine Smith, Inc., 1976, p. 192-3; **97 L, C, and R:** Franklin D. Roosevelr Library, National Archives; **97 LR and 98 L:** Tribune Media Services Inc. Reprinted with permission; **98 R:** Geisburg Collection, Prints Division, New York Public Library, Astor, Lenox and Tilden Foundations; **100:** © 1936 *New York News,* Inc., Pulitzer Prize Collection, Columbia University; **101 L:** LC 34315; **101** C: LC 86603; **101 R:** LC 85953,Swann Collection; **102 L:** Reprinted courtesy of Bill Mauldin, *What's Got up Your Back,* New York: Harper, 1961, cover; **102 C:** Reprinted courtesy of Bill Mauldin, *Up Front,* New York: WW. Norton and Co., 1991, p.59; **102 R, 103 L, C, R:** Reprinted courtesy of Bill Mauldin, *Back Home,* New York: Wm. Sloan Associates, 1947, pp.13, 187, 226, 229; **104 L:** © St. Louis Post-Dispatch. *Taking Liberty with the Lady,* Nashville: Eagle Nest Publishing, 1986, p.l 15; **104 R:** Reprinted courtesy of

Bill Mauldin; **105:** *Herblock: A Cartoonist's Life.* New York: Macmillan, 1993, p. 142; **106 L:** Tribune Media Services Inc. Reprinted with permission. Dwight D. Eisenhower Library, National Archives; **106 UR:** © St. Louis Post-Dispatch. *As I Saw It,* New York: Simon and Schuster, 1953; **106 LR:** Courtesy of Bernarda Shahn. Collection New Jersey State Museum; **107 L and R:** *Herblock: A Cartoonist's Life.* New York: Macmillan, 1993, p. 134, 166; **108:** LC 34209; **109 L:** LC 116028; **110:** Reprinted with permission. Toronto Star Syndicate. *Taking Liberty with the Lady,* Nashville: Eagle Nest Publishing, 1986, p. 115; **111 UL:** LC 39623; **111 LL:** Library of Congress; **111 R:** © 1961 E.G. Publications, Inc. All rights reserved. Used with Permission. "A Day with JFK," Mad Magazine #67; **112 L:** Reprinted courtesy of Bill Mauldin, John E Kennedy Library, National Archives; **112 R:** Reprinted courtesy of Bill Mauldin; **113:** © Jules Feiffer; **114 U and L:** © 1967 Pat Oliphant. Reprinted courtesy of Susan Conway Gallery; **115 UR:** © 1968 Pat Oliphant. Reprinted courtesy of Susan Conway Gallery; **115 LR:** © 1970 Pat Oliphant. Reprinted courtesy of Susan Conway Gallery; **116:** © Jules Feiffer; **117:** Tribune Media Services Inc. Reprinted with permission; **118 L:** Lyndon B. Johnson Library, National Archives; **118 UR:** © Paul Szep. LC 82941, Swann Collection; **118 LR:** © Draper Hill. Reprinted with permission of *Worcester Telegram.* Lyndon B. Johnson Library, National Archives; **119 L:** © Paul Szep. LC 82942, Swann Collection; **119 R:** © Edward Sorel. *Superpen,* New York: Random House, 1978; **120 L:** © Paul Szep; **120 R:** © Jules Feiffer; **121 L, C, R:** *Herblock: A Cartoonist's Life.* New York: Macmillan, 1993, pp.143, 231, 242; **122 UL, LL, and R:** © 1973 *Los Angeles Times* Syndicate. Reprinted with permission. *The King and Us,* Los Angeles: Clymer Publications, 1974, 1975, pp. 45, 21, 137; **123 UL:** © 1973 Pat Oliphant. Re-printed courtesy of Susan Conway Gallery; **123 LL:** *Herblock: A Cartoonist's Life.* New York: Macmillan, 1993, p.246; **123 R:** © 1984 Pat Oliphant. Reprinted courtesy of Susan Conway Gallery; **124 UL:** © Tony Auth. Reprinted by permission of Universal Press Syndicate. *Behind the Lines,* Boston: Houghton Mifflin Co., 1977; **124 LL:** © Doug Marlette. *The Emperor Has No Clothes,* Washington, D.C.: Graphic Press, 1976, p.34; **124 UR:** Mike Peters, © 1972 *Dayton Daily News. The Nixon Chronicles,* Dayton: Lorenz Press, Inc. 1976; **124 LR:** Tribune Media Services Inc. Reprinted with permission. *The 1970s Best Political Cartoons of the Decade,* New York: McGraw-Hill Book Co., 1981, p.70; **125:** © 1973 G. B. Trudeau. Reprinted by permission of Universal Press Syndicate; **126:** © 1974 Pat Oliphant. Reprinted courtesy of Susan Conway Gallery; **127:** © 1978 *Los Angeles Times.* Distributed by *Los Angeles Times Syndicate.* Reprinted with permission. *Conartist,* Los Angeles: *Los Angeles Times,* 1993, p.175; **128 L:** Mike Peters, c. 1976; *Dayton Daily News. On the Edge,* Dayton: DNI Publishing, 1994, p.18; **128 R:** © Doug Marlette. *Drawing Blood,* Washington: Graphic Press, 1980, p.15; **129 UL:** ©Jerry Robinson. Reprinted by permission Cartoonists and Writers Syndicate. *The 1970s Best Political Cartoons of the Decade,* New York: McGraw-Hill Book Co., 1981, p. 162; **129 LL:** © Jim Borgman. Reprinted with the special permission of King Features Syndicate. *Smorgasborgman,* Cincinnati: Armadillo Press, 1982, p.20; **129 UR:** © Doug Marlette. *Drawing Blood,* Washington: Graphic Press, 1980, p.34; **129 LR:** © Jim Borgman. Reprinted with the special permission of King Features Syndicate, *Smorgasborgman,* Cincinnati: Armadillo Press, 1982, p.39; **130:** Tribune Media Services Inc. Reprinted with permission; **131 UL:** Tribune Media Services Inc. Reprinted with permission. *Wright Side Up,* New York: Simon & Shuster, 1981, p.204; **131 LL:** Tribune Media Services Inc. Reprinted with permission; **131 R:** © David Levine, LC 105502; **132 L:** © 1978 *Los Angeles Times.* Distributed by *Los Angeles Times Syndicate.* Reprinted with permission. *Conartist,* Los Angeles: *Los Angeles Times,* 1993, p. 103; **132 R:** © Doug Marlette. *Shred This Book,* Atlanta: Peachtree Publishers, LTD, 1988, p. 16; **133:** Tribune Media Services Inc. Reprinted with permission. *Wright Side Up,* New York: Simon & Shuster, 1981, p. 24; **134 R:** © Jim Borgman. Reprinted with the special permission of King Features Syndicate. *The Great Communicator,* Cincinnati: Colloquial Books, 1985, p.143; **134 L:** © Bill Day. *Day-Ja Vu,* Detroit: Detroit Free Press, 1988; **135 L:** © TomToles. Reprinted by permission of Universal Press Syndicate; **135 R:** © Paul Szep; **136:** © Jim Borgman. Reprinted with the special permission of King Features Syndicate. *Disturbing the Peace,* Cincinnati: Colloquial Books, 1995, p.64; **137 U:** © Michael Ramirez, *Memphis Commercial Appeal* Reprinted by permission Copley News Service; **137 L:** Tribune Media Services Inc. Reprinted with permission; **138 L:** © Jim Borgman. Reprinted with the special permission of King Features Syndicate. *Disturbing the Peace,* Cincinnati: Colloquial Books, 1995, p.48; **138 R:** © Kevin Kallaugher, *Baltimore Sun.* Reprinted by permission of Cartoonists and Writers Syndicate. *Kaltoons: A Collection of Political Cartoons from The Baltimore Sun,* Baltimore: Chatsworth Press, 1992, p. 136; **139 U:** © 1991 *Fort Worth Star-Telegram.* Courtesy of Etta Hulme. *Best Editorial Cartoons of the Year, 1992 Edition,* Gretna, Louisiana: Pelican Publishing Co, 1992, p.8; **139 R:** Mike Peters, © 1990 *Dayton Daily News,* United Features Syndicate, Inc.; **140 L:** © Kevin Kallaugher, *Baltimore Sun.* Reprinted by permission of Cartoonists and Writers Syndicate. *Kaltoons: A Collection of Political Cartoons from The Baltimore Sun,* p.94; **140 R:** ©Tony Auth. Reprinted by permission of Universal Press Syndicate; **141:** © *Christian Science Monitor,* **142 UL:** Tribune Media Services Inc. Reprinted with permission. *The 1970s Best Political Cartoons of the Decade,* New York: McGraw-Hill Book Co., 1981, p. 183; **142LL:** ©Signe Wilkinson. Reprinted by permission of Cartoonists and Writers Syndicate. *Abortion Cartoons on Demand,* Philadelphia: Broad Street Books, 1992; **142 UR:** © 1982 Doug Marlette. *Shred This Book,* Atlanta: Peachtree Publishers, LTD, 1988, p.81; **142 LR:** Mike Peters, © 1983 *Dayton Daily News. Happy Days Are Here Again,* New York: Topper Books, 1992; **143:** Mike Peters, © 1991 *Dayton Daily News,* United Features Syndicate, Inc. *Happy Days Are Here Again,* New York: Topper Books, 1992; **144:** © 1992 G. B. Trudeau. Reprinted by permission of Universal Press Syndicate; **145 UL:** Tribune Media Services Inc. Reprinted with permission; **145 LL:** © Tom Toles. Reprinted by permission of Universal Press Syndicate; **145 R:** *Herblock: A Cartoonist's Life.* New York: Macmillan, 1993, p.340; **146 U:** Tribune Media Services Inc. Reprinted with permission; **146 L;** © 1995 Pat Oliphant. Reprinted by permission of Universal Press Syndicate. Courtesy of Susan Conway Gallery; **147 U:** Tribune Media Services Inc. Reprinted with permission; **147 L:** © Steve Benson. Reprinted by permission of United Feature Syndicate, Inc.; **148:** © Signe Wilkinson. Reprinted by permission of Cartoonists and Writers Syndicate; **149:** ©2008 Gordon Campbell; **150:** ©2005 Nick Anderson Used with the permission of Nick Anderson and the Washington Post Writers Group in conjunction with the Cartoonist Group. All rights reserved; **151UL:** © David Horsey, **151UL:** © 1996 *Seattle Post-Intelligencer;* **151LR:** : © 1996 *Seattle Post-Intelligencer;*

152: © 2000 Kevin Kallaugher, *The Economist,* Kaltoons LLC, New York Times Syndicate; **153 UL:** © 2002 Mike Ritter. King Features Syndicate; **153 UR:** © 2000 Jeff Danziger, New York Times Service; **153 LR:** © 2000 Ann Telnaes. Reprinted by permission of Cartoonist Group; **154 L:** © 2001 Mike Luckovich. Used with the permission of Mike Luckovich and Creators Syndicate, Inc. All rights reserved; **154 R:** © 2001 Tribune Media Services, Inc All Rights Reserved. Reprinted with permission. **155 L:** © 2001 Mike Ritter. King Features Syndicate; **155 R:** © 2001 Grimmy, Inc. Distributed by King Features Syndicate, Inc.; **156:** © 2001 The Christian Science Monitor (www.csmonitor.com). All rights reserved; **157 L:** © Clay Bennett**; 157 UR:** © 2001 The Christian Science Monitor (www.csmonitor.com). All rights reserved; **157 LR** © 2001 By permission of Michael Ramirez and Creators Syndicate, Inc.; **158 UL:** © 2001 By permission of John Deering and Creators Syndicate Inc.; **158 UR:** © 2002 Mike Luckovich. Used with the permission of Mike Luckovich and Creators Syndicate Inc.; Inc. All rights reserved; **158 LL:** © 2002 Jim Borgman, *Cincinnati Inquirer.* Reprinted by permission of UNIVERSAL UCLICK. All rights reserved; **158 LR:** Ed Gamble. © 2002 *Florida Times-Union.* With permission of King Features Syndicate. **159:** © 2002 By permission of Michael Ramirez and Creators Syndicate, Inc; **160 L:** © 2003 *Seattle Post-Intelligencer*; **160 R:** © 2002 Jeff Stahler; **161 L:** © 2003 Frank Cammuso, *Post-Standard, Syracuse, NY;* **161 R:** Auth © 2003 *The Philadelphia Inquirer.* Reprinted by permission of UNIVERSAL UCLICK. All rights reserved; **162 L:** By permission of Chris Britt and Creators Syndicate, Inc.; **162 R:** © Tribune Media Services, Inc. All Rights Reserved. Reprinted with permission; **163 L:** © 2006 Ann Telnaes, Reprinted by permission of Cartoonist Group; **162 UR** © 2003 Ann Telnaes. Reprinted by permission of Cartoonist Group; **162 LR:** © Ann Telnaes. Reprinted by permission of Cartoonist Group; **164: ©** 2004 RJ Matson. *The New York Observer*; **165:** © 2005 Jeff Danziger. New York Times Service*;* **166 L:** © 2007 Mike Keefe, *The Denver Post*; **166 R:** Doonesbury © 2004 G.B. Trudeau. Reprinted by permission of UNIVERSAL UCLICK. All rights reserved; **167 L:** Tom Toles. © 2006 *The Washington Post.* Reprinted by permission of Universal Press Syndicate, *Washington Post*; **167 UR:** Tom Toles. © 2004 *The Washington Post.* Reprinted by permission of UNIVERSAL UCLICK. All rights reserved; **167 LR:** © Tom Toles; **168:** ©2004 Kirk Anderson, kirktoons.com; **169 L:** © 2006 Ted Rall, Reprinted by permission of Universal Press Syndicate; 16**9 R:** © Ted Rall; **170:** © 2007 Mikhaela Reid; *Attack of the 50ft. Mikhaela*; **171:** © 2007 Matt Wuerker. www.politico.com/wuerrker; **172 UL:** © 2007 Walt Handelsman, *www.newsday.com*; **172 UR:** © 2006 Kevin Kallaugher, Kaltoons LLC; **172 LL:** © 2008 Ann Telnaes, *www.washingtonpost.com*; **172 LR:** © 2007 Mark Fiore, www.markfiore.com; **174:** *The Boondocks* © 2001 Aaron McGruder. Reprinted by permission of UNIVERSAL UCLICK. All rights reserved; **175U:** Lalo © 2003 Lalo Alcaraz. Reprinted by permission of UNIVERSAL UCLICK. All rights reserved; **175L:** La Cucaracha © 1998 Lalo Alcaraz. Reprinted by permission of UNIVERSAL UCLICK. All rights reserved; **176 UL:** Michael Ramirez: **176 LR:** By permission of Michael Ramirez and Creators Syndicate, Inc; **177 UL:** © 2006 *The Chattanooga Times.* All rights re served by Bruce Plante; **177 LR:** © By permission of Steve Benson and Creators Syndicate, Inc; **178 UL:** © 2005 Mike Luckovich. Used with the permission of Mike Luckovich and Creators Syndicate, Inc. All rights reserved; **178 LR:** © 2006 Tribune Media Services, Inc. All Rights Reserved. Reprinted with permission; **179 LL:** Carlson © 2005 *Milwaukee-Journal Sentinel.* Reprinted by permission of UNIVERSAL UCLICK . All rights reserved; **179 UR:** © 2005 Nick Anderson. Reprinted by permission of Cartoonist Group and *Courier-Journal,* (Louisville), 2005; **180 UL:** © 2009 Signe Wilkinson. Used with the permission of Signe Wilkinson, the Washington Post Writers Group and the Cartoonist Group. All rights reserved.; **180 UR:** © Tribune Media Services, Inc. All Rights Reserved. Reprinted with permission; **180 LL:** © 2009 Steve Kelley. Used with the permission of Steve Kelley and the Cartoonist Group. All rights reserved; **181 UL:** © 1983 Jim Borgman. *Cincinnati Inquirer.* Reprinted by permission of UNIVERSAL UCLICK. All rights reserved; **181 UR:** © 2008 Sandy Huffaker, www.huffakerart.com; **181 LR:** © 2007 Nick Anderson. Used with the permission of Nick Anderson and the Washington Post Writers Group in conjunction with the Cartoonist Group. All rights reserved; **182 L:** By permission of Michael Ramirez and Creators Syndicate, Inc.*;* **182 R:** © 2008 *Seattle Post-Intelligencer;* **183 UL:** © Tribune Media Services, Inc. All Rights Reserved. Reprinted with permission; **183 UR.** © 2008 Daryl Cagle, MSNBC, and *PoliticalCartoons.com*; **183 LL:** © Tribune Media Services, Inc. All Rights Reserved. Reprinted with permission; **184 L:** © 2008 Signe Wilkinson. Used with the permission of Signe Wilkinson, the Washington Post Writers Group and the Cartoonist Group. All rights reserved;**184 R:** © 2008 Joel Pett, *Lexington Herald–Leader*, Cartoonists and Writers Syndicate; **185:** © 2008 Clay Bennett. Used with the permission of Clay Bennett and the Washington Post Writers Group in conjunction with the Cartoonist Group. All rights reserved; **203:** Auth © 1976 *The Philadelphia Inquirer.* Reprinted by permission of UNIVERSAL UCLICK. All rights reserved.

INDEX